Items should be returned on or before the last date shown below. Items not already requested by other borrowers may be renewed in person, in writing or by telephone. To renew, please quote the number on the barcode label. To renew online a PIN is required. This can be requested at your local library.
Renew online @ **www.dublincitypubliclibraries.ie**
Fines charged for overdue items will include postage incurred in recovery. Damage to or loss of items will be charged to the borrower.

Leabharlanna Poiblí Chathair Bhaile Átha Cliath
Dublin City Public Libraries

Baile Átha Cliath
Dublin City

Date Due	Date Due	Date Due
2 0 JUN 2018 2017 -8 FEB		3 0 JAN 2018

GOOD NEWS BIBLE

Collins
SINCE 1819

BIBLE SOCIETY

GOOD NEWS BIBLE

The Bible Societies/Collins, a division of HarperCollinsPublishers

First edition © 1979
Second edition © 1995
Third edition © 2004
This edition © 2014

Title	Code	ISBN
Sunrise, hardback	GNB 043P SR	978-0-00-748012-8
Sunrise, paperback	GNB 040P SR	978-0-00-748014-2
Rainbow, hardback	GNB 043P CD	978-0-00-748011-1
New Life, hardback	GNB 043P CHY	978-0-00-748013-5

Text design by Colin Hall
Typesetting and production management by Bible Society Resources Ltd,
a wholly-owned subsidary of The British and Foreign Bible Society
To find out more about the Good News Bible visit: **bibleresources.org.uk**
To find out more about the work of Bible Society visit: **biblesociety.org.uk**

BSRL/70M/2014
Printed in China

The British and Foreign Bible Society is a member of the United Bible Societies
which is a worldwide fellowship of National Bible Societies working in more than
180 countries. Their aim is to achieve the widest possible, effective and meaningful
distribution of the Holy Scriptures, and to help people interact with the Word of God.
More than 500 million Scriptures are distributed every year. You are invited to share in
this work by your prayers and gifts. The Bible Society in your country will be very happy
to provide details of its activity.

Contents

Books of the Bible in alphabetical order

Other Abbreviations

Circa (around)	c
Old Testament	OT
New Testament	NT
Septuagint	LXX

Welcome to the Good News Bible

The Good News Bible is an easy-to-read translation of the Bible. It uses clear, readable, everyday English, which is why, over the years, thousands of churches and schools and millions of individuals have chosen the Good News Bible.

The Bible is an anthology

The Bible is not one book, but a collection of books bound into one volume. (In fact, that's where it gets its name from. The Bible is the English-language version of the Greek words *ta biblia*, which means "the books".) Written over thousands of years, by many different authors, these books contain many different types of writing: poetry, history, laws, prophecy, proverbs and sayings, stories, letters and many more.

This Bible is in two parts

These books are arranged into two sections: the Old and New Testaments. Testament means "promise". For Christians the "Old Testament" is the promise given by God to the Jews; the "New Testament" is the promise given through Jesus.

The Hebrew Scriptures or Old Testament (39 books)

The first part of the Bible contains the sacred writings of Judaism. This tells the story of the people of Israel. The Jewish name for this is the *Tanakh* : the name is based on the first letters of the three main sections: *Torah* ("The Law"), *Nevi'im* ("The Prophets") and *Ketuvim* ("The Writings"). TNK = *Tanakh*.

Christians call this section the **Old Testament**, which is arranged as follows:

The Law The first five books tell the story of the creation of the world, God's promises to people like Abraham and Jacob, the beginnings of the Israelite nation, their slavery in Egypt and their escape. It also contains the Law which the Jewish people were supposed to obey.

Historical books Twelve books covering the history of Israel, from the conquest of the Promised Land, to the defeat, exile and eventual return.

Poetic books Six extremely varied books reflecting all the moods of human life. They address many fundamental and difficult issues of human existence such as suffering, joy, love, anger, despair, delight and everything in between!

Prophets Sixteen books, the first four of which are the major prophets (which really means long books) while the remaining twelve are the minor prophets (they're shorter). They cover the time from the later kings into the exile. But they also contain prophecies of the future, and many statements which Christians believe were fulfilled in Jesus.

The Christian Scriptures or New Testament (27 books)

This is the collection of Christian Scriptures. These writings fall into three main groups:

The Gospels and Acts The four Gospels are a biographical and historical look at the life of Jesus, while the book of Acts tells the story of the first thirty years of the Early Church.

Letters of Paul, John, Peter and others. These were circulated among the first followers of Jesus. They give guidance, encouragement and sometimes a strong rebuke to the first communities of Christians.

Prophecy This was probably sent as a letter, but, with its visionary, apocalyptic language, stands alone.

Finding your way around

To help readers find their way around, each book of the Bible is subdivided into chapters and verses. So when people talk about a Bible reference, they are talking about this system. John 3.16 is like an address: it means the book of John, chapter 3 and then verse 16.

The books of the Bible did not originally include chapters and verses. These were added a lot later. The chapter numbering system we use today dates from the 13th century AD, and the verse subdivisions date from the 16th century.

section of the Bible you are in (see page v)

name of the book you are in plus the chapters that appear on that page

page number

* at end of the word indicates there is more information in the notes at the foot of the column

* at the start of the word indicates a cross reference at the foot of the column

chapter number

numbers in bold, e.g. 27.13, point to the chapter and verse

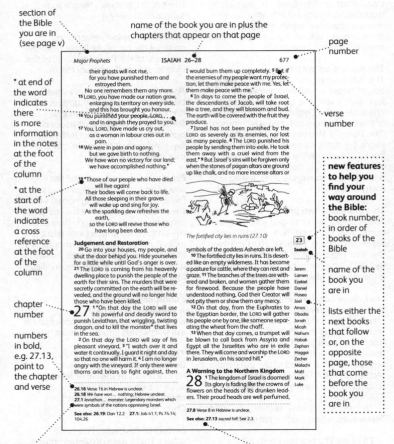

Major Prophets   ISAIAH 26–28   677

their ghosts will not rise,
for you have punished them and estroyed them.
No one remembers them any more. **15** LORD, you have made our nation grow, enlarging its territory on every side, and this has brought you honour. **16** You punished your people, LORD, and in anguish they prayed to you. **17** You, LORD, have made us cry out, as a woman in labour cries out in pain. **18** We were in pain and agony, but we gave birth to nothing. We have won no victory for our land; we have accomplished nothing.*

19 *Those of our people who have died will live again! Their bodies will come back to life. All those sleeping in their graves will wake up and sing for joy. As the sparkling dew refreshes the earth, so the LORD will revive those who have long been dead.

Judgement and Restoration
20 Go into your houses, my people, and shut the door behind you. Hide yourselves for a little while until God's anger is over. **21** The LORD is coming from his heavenly dwelling place to punish the people of the earth for their sins. The murders that were secretly committed on the earth will be revealed, and the ground will no longer hide those who have been killed.

27 **1** "On that day the LORD will use his powerful and deadly sword to punish Leviathan, that wriggling, twisting dragon, and to kill the monster* that lives in the sea.

2 On that day the LORD will say of his pleasant vineyard, **3** "I watch over it and water it continually. I guard it night and day so that no one will harm it. **4** I am no longer angry with the vineyard. If only there were thorns and briars to fight against, then

I would burn them up completely. **5** But if the enemies of my people want my protection, let them make peace with me. Yes, let them make peace with me."

6 In days to come the people of Israel, the descendants of Jacob, will take root like a tree, and they will blossom and bud. The earth will be covered with the fruit they produce.

7 Israel has not been punished by the LORD as severely as its enemies, nor lost as many people. **8** The LORD punished his people by sending them into exile. He took them away with a cruel wind from the east. **9** But Israel's sins will be forgiven only when the stones of pagan altars are ground up like chalk, and no more incense altars or

The fortified lies in ruins (27.10)

symbols of the goddess Asherah are left.

10 The fortified city lies in ruins. It is deserted like an empty wilderness. It has become a pasture for cattle, where they can rest and graze. **11** The branches of the trees are withered and broken, and women gather them for firewood. Because the people have understood nothing, God their Creator will not pity them or show them any mercy.

12 On that day, from the Euphrates to the Egyptian border, the LORD will gather his people one by one, like someone separating the wheat from the chaff. **13** When that day comes, a trumpet will be blown to call back from Assyria and Egypt all the Israelites who are in exile there. They will come and worship the LORD in Jerusalem, on his sacred hill.*

A Warning to the Northern Kingdom
28 **1** The kingdom of Israel is doomed! Its glory is fading like the crowns of flowers on the heads of its drunken leaders. Their proud heads are well perfumed,

26.16 Verse 16 in Hebrew is unclear.
26.18 *We have won… nothing;* Hebrew unclear.
27.1 *leviathan… monster:* Legendary monsters which were symbols of the nations oppressing Israel.

See also: 26.19: Dan 12.2 **27.1:** Job 41.1; Ps 74.14; 104.26

27.8 Verse 8 in Hebrew is unclear.

See also: 27.13 *sacred hill:* See 2.3.

23
Isaiah

Jerem
Lamen
Ezekiel
Daniel
Hosea
Joel
Amos
Obadia
Jonah
Micah
Nahum
Habak
Zephan
Haggai
Zecher
Malachi
Matt
Mark
Luke

new features to help you find your way around the Bible:
book number, in order of books of the Bible

name of the book you are in

lists either the next books that follow or, on the opposite page, those that come before the book you are in

verse number

footnotes – provide information on the meaning of the text; textual notes on the translation and alternative understandings of the meanings of the original text

cross references guide you to other passages where identical or similar matters or ideas are dealt with

How to read the Bible

Take your time
Read slowly and carefully. The Bible wasn't built for speed reading. Try to read in "chunks". One verse on its own might not make much sense, but when you read a bit more of the text around it, that can really help. You need to read enough of the passage to get an idea of what the overall story or argument is. Sometimes it really helps to read the passage out loud. And the Bible was meant to be heard this way. For most of its history it was more of an audiobook: because most people couldn't read or write, they had the passage read to them. And because it's such an accessible translation, the Good News Bible is great for this!

Work to a plan
Q: How do you eat an elephant? A: One bite at a time.
The Bible is a seriously complex book. You can't expect to read the whole thing through at one sitting. Instead you have to break it down and read it in bite-sized chunks.

It helps to have a plan. Maybe you want to work through a book, chapter by chapter. Maybe, if the book is shorter you can read through the whole book. Or maybe you want to use a specific reading plan to help you explore what the Bible has to say on a particular topic, character or event. There are plenty of reading plans available to help you.

Always ask questions
One of the most important tools to help you read the Bible is your brain. Ask who, why, what, where, when? Who is saying this? Why is this happening? When is this story set? Who is this person? What does that mean? Sometimes it helps to make notes as you go along. You can draw pictures and diagrams if that helps.

Try to work out what type of writing it is
As we have seen, the Bible is a mixture of different types of writing: there are laws and letters, stories, poems and proverbs. And you don't read all of these in the same way. You don't read a poem in the same way as you read a historical account. So try to ask yourself "What type of writing is this?" That will be a big help in understanding how you should read the passage.

Explore the history and culture
You've been asking questions? Good. Now you have to find the answers! In the story of the Good Samaritan, for example, it really helps to understand the fact that Jews and Samaritans didn't like each other. A lot of the answers will be in the text. But sometimes it helps to get a good Bible guide to give you the background on the history, culture and customs of the Old and New Testaments.

Don't worry
The Bible is a very old book written in a different culture and at a different time. There is a lot of stuff in it that is confusing to a modern reader. So don't worry if there are bits you don't understand or names you can't pronounce! Just move on. Concentrate on the bits you do understand.

Pray as you go
Christians believe that the Bible is more than just another book – it's the Word of God. And God speaks to us through it. So as you go along, listen out for him. Pray before you start reading. When you come to think about what you've read, ask yourself, "What is God saying to me through this?"

Don't think it's not for you!
Reading the Bible is not something just for experts. It's for everyone. Throughout history ordinary men, women and children have been inspired, challenged, thrilled and transformed by the Bible. They weren't any different to us. All they had that was different was the desire to read the Bible for themselves.

So give it a try! You never know what's waiting there for you!

The big picture: 20 must-read passages

The Bible is full of great stories, inspirational writing and life-changing information. The passages below are a good place to start.

The story of creation (Genesis 1—2)

The beginning. God creates the universe, the earth, sun, moon, all the animals and, of course, people.
Why is this important?
- It shows who made the world and universe.
- It shows what humanity's relationship with God and the rest of creation should be like.

Human disobedience (Genesis 3)

Adam and Eve disobey God and are banished from the garden of Eden.
Why is this important?
- It shows how evil entered the world.
- It demonstrates that all of us have a choice whether to follow God or not.

Noah and the flood (Genesis 6—7)

Noah and his family gather all the animals into a huge boat, while God sends an enormous flood.
Why is this important?
- It shows God is a God of judgment as well as mercy.
- It shows God's promise never to destroy the earth again.
- It shows God is concerned for all his creation and not just for human beings.
- It introduces the 'forty days' theme, which runs throughout the Bible.

The covenant (Genesis 17)

God promises Abraham that he will be the father of a great nation.
Why is this important?
- It introduces the covenant – the promise between God and his people.
- It introduces us to Abraham, the great man of faith and ancestor of Israel.
- It starts the story of the nation of Israel – the people who were to descend from Abraham.

God meets Moses (Exodus 3)

In the desert, God appears to Moses in the form of a burning bush. God tells Moses that his name is "I AM".
Why is this important?
- It introduces the Old Testament name of God – Yahweh.
- It shows God's special relationship with Moses.
- It reminds us of God's promise to rescue Israel.

The passover (Exodus 11.1—13.16)

God punishes the king of Egypt and rescues his people from slavery.
Why is this important?
- It shows how God rescued Israel from Egypt.
- It introduces the Passover – a Jewish festival still celebrated today.

The ten commandments
(Deuteronomy 5)

God gives Moses the Ten Commandments which sum up what God expects of God's people.
Why is this important?
- The commandments form the basis of most of the world's legal systems.
- They form the basis of "the Law" – the rules which focused Israel on God.

The Lord is my shepherd (Psalm 23)

One of the best-loved and most famous passages in the Bible, this poem is a powerful image of God's care and love.
Why is this important?
- It's one of the most beautiful poems ever written.
- It sums up the caring, personal aspect of God.
- It shows us the idea of God as a shepherd – an image later used by Jesus.

The suffering servant (Isaiah 53)

Isaiah is a book which features many passages about the Messiah. This shows us a suffering, ill-treated servant, who is hated, rejected and sacrificed, although innocent.
Why is this important?
- It's a key prophecy about the Messiah – the "anointed one" who will rescue Israel.
- Christians interpret this as a clear prophecy of Jesus, and his sacrificial death.

The birth of Jesus (Luke 1.23—2.39)

It's the story of Jesus' birth into a peasant household and how the good news is given first to poor shepherds, sitting out on the dark hills. This is good news for everyone.
Why is this important?
- It describes the birth of Jesus.
- It shows how Jesus came to an ordinary family in an extraordinary way.

- It's the root of the Christian festival of Christmas.

The baptism of Jesus (Matthew 3)

Jesus is baptized by John. The Spirit of God descends on him and a voice is heard from heaven.
Why is this important?
- It shows the beginning of Jesus' ministry.
- It introduces us to the work of John the Baptist.
- It shows the origin of the Christian practice of baptism.
- It hints at the Christian concept of the Trinity.

The sermon on the mount
(Matthew 5—7)

It's not really a sermon – that title comes from a lot later, but this is a core collection of Jesus' teaching and sayings on subjects such as love, forgiveness, money and behaviour.
Why is this important?
- It's Jesus' manifesto – his programme for the kingdom of God.
- It contains what are sometimes called the Beatitudes – Jesus' declaration of who is truly happy and blessed.
- It contains the core ethical and moral beliefs of the Christian faith.

The lost son (Luke 15.11—32)

The story of a son who leaves home, loses everything and yet still is welcomed back.
Why is this important?
- It shows Jesus' message of forgiveness.
- It demonstrates the fatherlike qualities of God.
- It's one of the best stories ever told!

The last supper
(Matthew 26.17—30)

The account of the meal which Jesus shared with his disciples the night before his death. He tells them that the bread is his "body" and the wine is his "blood" and asks that the disciples eat and drink these in memory of him.

Why is this important?

- It reminds Jesus' followers of the sacrifice he made for them.
- The account is the basis for the Eucharist or Communion which is celebrated by most Christians.

The death of Jesus (Matthew 27)

The account of how Jesus was executed by the Roman authorities and what happened in the hours surrounding his death.

Why is this important?

- It shows the earth-shattering effects of Jesus' death.
- It introduces the cross – one of the key symbols of Christianity.
- It shows how people of the time reacted to Jesus' execution.

The resurrection of Jesus (Luke 24)

This is an account of Jesus' return from the dead and his subsequent appearances to his disciples.

Why is this important?

- It tells of Jesus' rising from the dead – the key event in the Christian religion.
- For Christians, it shows that Jesus was who he said he was: the Son of God.
- It depicts the most important event in history!

The coming of the Holy Spirit (Acts 2)

Jesus promised his disciples the Holy Spirit. The Spirit gives the disciples courage to speak out and is accompanied by powerful signs. This is the beginning of the Church.

Why is this important?

- It shows how the Early Church put Jesus' teaching to work.
- It introduces the Holy Spirit – the power behind the Church.

- It's the origin of the Christian festival of Pentecost.

Faith makes us right with God (Romans 5.1—11)

A passage which sums up the core message of Romans: it is through faith in Jesus that we are put right with God.

Why is this important?

- Paul explains that faith in God is what really counts.
- This passage shows how we cannot be saved in our own power – only through God.

Paul talks about love (1 Corinthians 13)

An inspirational passage about the power of love – the greatest thing of all. Without love, says Paul, our words are nothing but noise.

Why is this important?

- It shows what really matters in life
- It's one of the greatest pieces of writing ever!
- It inspires us all to act in a truly loving way.

Alpha and Omega (Revelation 21)

It's the end … and the beginning. This passage brings the story of the Bible round in a kind of arc – we started with the creation of the earth and the heavens and we end with the creation of a new heaven and a new earth where God and his people will live together. There will be food for all, healing for all, peace for all.

Why is this important?

- It shows us God's final victory over death, sadness and pain.
- It brings us back to the beginning – but with a new heaven and earth.
- It shows a picture of what is going to happen in the future.

The Christian year

The Christian year is divided up with events which remind us of events in the life of Jesus. It begins in late November with Advent, which prepares us for Christmas – the birth of Christ. After that we move through Lent, towards Holy Week and Easter, which commemorate the death and resurrection of Jesus. Then it is on to Pentecost and the founding of the Church. And then there are other festivals which remind us of various important figures or aspects of Christianity. Some festivals, like Christmas Day, happen on the same date every year, while others move around within a range of dates.

Advent
The start of the Christian year, Advent is a four-week period leading up to Christmas. See Isaiah 40.1–11; Micah 5.2–5; Luke 1.26–38.

Christmas Day
This is the day when Christians celebrate Jesus' birth. See Matthew 1; Luke 2.1–21.

Epiphany
Twelve days after Christmas day, this celebrates the visit of the wise men to Jesus. See Matthew 2.1–15.

Lent
Lent is the forty-day period before Easter. It begins on Ash Wednesday. The period of forty days reflects the time Jesus spent in the wilderness. See Matthew 4.1–11; Mark 1.9–13; Luke 4.1–13.

Easter and Holy Week
Easter is the most important festival in the Christian year.

- **Palm Sunday** is the sixth and last Sunday of Lent. This commemorates Jesus' entry into Jerusalem and marks the start of Holy Week. See Matthew 21.1–11; Mark 11.1–11; Luke 19.28–40; John 12.12–19.

- **Maundy Thursday** commemorates the Last Supper, when Jesus washed the feet of his disciples and instituted the Eucharist. See Matthew 26.17–30; Mark 14.12–26; Luke 22.7–23 John 13.1–20; 1 Corinthians 11.23–25.

- **Good Friday** is a solemn day on which Christians remember Jesus' death. See Matthew 27; Mark 15; Luke 23; John 18.28–19.42.

- **Easter Sunday** is the culmination of Holy Week and celebrates the resurrection of Jesus Christ. See Matthew 28; Mark 16.1–8; Luke 24; John 20; 1 Corinthians 15.3–7.

Ascension Day
This commemorates the ascension of Jesus into heaven forty days after his resurrection from the dead. See Luke 24.50–53; Acts 1.6–11.

Pentecost
This is the seventh Sunday after Easter and commemorates the coming of the Holy Spirit. It's the birthday of the Church. See Acts 2.1–42.

Hebrew Bible/Jewish festivals

The Hebrew calendar follows a lunar cycle, linked to the rhythm of the solar year by the addition of an extra month every two to three years to keep the two in close correspondence.

- **Shabbat**, the weekly Sabbath, is the most important 'festival', a day of rest, mindfulness, study and community.

The main annual festivals are:

- **Passover, or Pesach**: This week-long, spring time **Festival of**

Unleavened Bread commemorates the deliverance of the Israelites from Egypt. On the first nights, families eat a special meal including unleavened bread and bitter herbs, over which they recount the story of the Exodus from Egypt. See Leviticus 23.4–8; Numbers 28.16–25

- **Pentecost** (**Shavuot**, or the Feast of Weeks) celebrates the Giving of the Torah to the Children of Israel on Mount Sinai, seven full weeks after the Exodus. It also marks the grain harvest. See Leviticus 23.15–22; Numbers 28.26–31.

- **The New Year**, **Rosh Hashanah**, takes place on the first two days of the seventh month. It is marked by solemn prayer and the sounding of the Shofar, the ram's horn.

- **The Day of Atonement, Yom Kippur**, on the tenth of the seventh month, is a day of fasting and repentance, when people ask forgiveness for their sins from each other and from God. See Leviticus 16; 23.23–32; Numbers 29.7–11.

- **Tabernacles**, or **Succot**, the Festival of Booths, in the same month, lasts for eight days and commemorates Israel's wanderings in the desert on their journey to the Promised Land. Families live in a Succah, or booth, which they decorate with branches

and fruits. See Leviticus 23.33–44; Numbers 29.12–40.

- **Hanukkah**, or the Feast of Lights, an eight-day festival, commemorates the purification of the Temple after the Maccabean victory over the Seleucid Greeks. The events are recorded in the Books of the Maccabees, written during the inter-testamental period.

- **Tu Bishevat**, the New Year for Trees, marks the beginning of spring in Israel and is a time to celebrate nature, and trees in particular.

- **Purim**, a joyful carnival festival, commemorates the rescue of the Jews in Persia as told in the Scroll of Esther. See Esther 9.20–32.

- **Yom Hashoah, Holocaust Memorial Day**, on the anniversary of the Warsaw Ghetto uprising, is devoted to remembering the victims of the Holocaust.

- **Yom Ha'atzmaut, Israel's independence day**, marks the date when the country was reborn, with the support of the United Nations, after two thousand years of Jewish exile.

- **Tishah Be'Av**, the Ninth of the month of Av, is a fast day commemorating the destruction of the first and second Temples, and numerous other tragedies.

The life of Jesus

At the heart of the Christian Bible is the figure of Jesus.

He was born into a poor family. After his birth the family spent some time as refugees. Little is known of his upbringing. For some fifteen years he followed his human father's trade, working as a carpenter and builder in Galilee.

Jesus was Jewish. In fact, he wasn't actually called Jesus – that is the Greek version of the Aramaic name *Yeshua* ('Joshua' in Hebrew). He was raised in a Jewish home, and circumcised as a boy; he was part of God's chosen people. God promised Abraham that a great blessing would come through his descendants, and Christians believe that Jesus is the fulfilment of that promise. He was brought up with a knowledge of Jewish law and tradition. He was called 'Rabbi' by some of his followers, which means teacher. He knew the Jewish Scriptures inside out. So much so that he managed to sum it all up in a few words.

When he was about thirty, he was baptized by his cousin John and, after a period in the wilderness, he began his public work.

From the start, **Jesus was a miracle worker**. Crowds flocked to him. He healed people, restored their sight and helped them to walk and there are three accounts of Jesus bringing people back to life. He fed thousands of people with a few loaves and fishes. He freed people from evil spirits. He was a man with power.

This power comes across in his words as well as his deeds. **Jesus was a teacher**. Above all it was said of him that he taught "with authority". But he didn't just talk at people: he engaged in debate and discussion, question and answer. Jesus was a storyteller: in fact, he never taught without using stories, known as parables. The stories grounded his teaching in everyday life. They were challenging and thought-provoking, and sometimes made people angry.

Perhaps the most persistent theme in his speaking and teaching was the "Kingdom of God". The Gospels mention the kingdom over eighty times and almost two-thirds of Jesus' parables take it as their subject. It was a kingdom that, to some extent, had already come – Jesus told his disciples to go out and tell people that the kingdom was at hand. But it was also a future kingdom. And **Jesus was the king**.

But if he was a king, he wasn't like the kings of this world. Far from driving out the Romans, Jesus told people to love their enemies. He preached forgiveness and peace. His kingdom was a kingdom of the oppressed, the outcast, the dispossessed, the desperate – all those who, as citizens, would usually be at the bottom of the pile in any earthly realm. In Jesus' kingdom, the poor were wealthy and enemies were friends.

In the end, this talk of kingdoms formed one of the main planks of the case for his execution. Stung by his criticism and appalled by his apparent blasphemy, the authorities closed in. His opponents accused him of claiming to be king of the Jews. After a final meal with his disciples, one of his friends betrayed him, and he was arrested. He was condemned to death. After being badly beaten he was crucified by the Roman authorities. Pilate even hung the phrase "King of the Jews" above him.

Three days later, strange rumours began. His followers claimed that he had risen from the dead. His tomb was empty. People started to see him on roads, in rooms, by the lakeside, in the cemetery. The news of his resurrection spread like wildfire. They thought they'd killed him – but he was more alive than ever.

The Life of Jesus:

- **The very beginning**: John 1.1

- **The birth of Jesus**: Luke 2.1–21

- **Baptism and temptation**: Luke 3.21–4.13

- **The work begins**: Mark 1.14–45

- **The life of the kingdom**: Matthew 5.1–48

- **How to pray**: Matthew 6.1–21

- **Walk the talk**: Matthew 6.22–7.29

- **Born again**: John 3.1–21

- **Food and water**: John 6.1–21

- **Who am I?**: Luke 8.22–38

- **Good samaritan**: Luke 10.25–37

- **Healing the sick**: Matthew 9

- **Being a disciple**: Luke 14.7–35

- **The great "I Am"**: John 8.12–59

- **Triumphal entry**: Matthew 21.1–11

- **The greatest commandment**: Matthew 22.34–46

- **Washing the feet**: John 13.1–20

- **The arrest**: Mark 14.27–72

- **The death** : Luke 23.13–56

- **Resurrection**: John 20.1–29

- **Back for good**: Matthew 28

How did we get the Bible?

The Bible was written and compiled over thousands of years. So how did that happen? Who wrote the Bible? And how was it put together?

It begins with stories

The Bible begins with the spoken word. That's how it was first passed on – as stories – tales of ancestors and heroes and their mysterious, powerful experiences of God. These formed the foundational stories about the Jewish people. They were preserved by the different tribes and carefully handed on from generation to generation. There were narratives like the story of Noah, for example; or poems like the song of Deborah in Judges (Judges 5). Or there were statements which the Israelites used in their religious services. In Deuteronomy 26, for example, Moses tells the Israelites that when they bring an offering they must recite a kind of "history" of who they are and where they came from. It begins *"My ancestor was a wandering Aramean, who took his family to Egypt to live…"* (Deuteronomy 26.5).

It was important to listen, learn, memorize and pass on these tales. In ancient cultures it was very important that they were handed on carefully. You had to do it right. But eventually the stories were written down. We don't know when, exactly – certainly some things were written down very early on. In Exodus, Moses records God's words as *"an account of this victory, so that it will be remembered"* (Exodus 17.14). And on Mount Sinai, the Law was engraved on *"two stone tablets on which God himself had written the commandments"* (Exodus 31.18).

Some of these books came directly from God in the form of prophecies: the book of Haggai, for example, collects prophecies spoken by Haggai on different dates. Sometimes they were compiled using a variety of sources – some of the history books mention other reference works, which are now lost.

The writings which came to form the Old Testament were written on scrolls and carefully copied from one generation to the next. And these came together to form the Hebrew Scriptures which Christians call the Old Testament.

The New Testament also begins with stories

In this case they were tales about Jesus, the things he did and said. They were remembered by the people who met him. And these people travelled from city to city, passing on what they had seen and heard.

These stories were carefully learnt and passed on. When Paul wrote to the Christians at Corinth he said "For I received from the Lord what I also passed on to you…" He passes on the things that he has been taught.

In the opening to his Gospel, Luke describes how he has carefully researched the story:

> Many people have done their best to write a report of the things that have taken place among us. They wrote what we have been told by those who saw these things from the beginning and who proclaimed the message. And so, your Excellency, because I have carefully studied all these matters from their beginning, I thought it would be good to write an orderly account for you. (Luke 1.1–3)

Luke has made his own investigation, but so have others. And these other reports have been based on the accounts of "those who saw these things from the beginning".

As well as the recollections and memories of eyewitnesses, there were probably written sources such as collections of Jesus' sayings and parables.

We know, though, that not everything Jesus said and did ended up in the Gospels. For example, Paul quotes a saying of Jesus: "There is more happiness in giving than in receiving" (Acts 20.35). But this saying doesn't appear in any of the Gospels. And in John's Gospel it says that "Jesus performed many other miracles which are not written down in this book" (John 20.30).

So the Gospels were carefully researched and compiled from various sources. But the base of all these accounts is the eyewitness accounts of the things that Jesus said and did.

The rest of the New Testament is made up of letters passed from church to church, written by leaders like Paul and James. But these also contain other kinds of early Christian writing. Philippians 2.5–11, for example, is a kind of hymn or poem, which

must have been used in the Early Church. Paul quotes it to remind the Philippians of who Jesus was and what he did.

These are, in fact, the earliest Christian documents that we have. They were probably written before the Gospels were compiled and date from the late AD 40s onwards. The letters would have been written on papyrus or sometimes parchment, which was then rolled up, put in a container and sent by a trusted courier to the recipients. If the letter was deemed important, once it had been read out to its recipients it would have been copied and passed on. In Paul's letter to the Colossians he tells them: "After you read this letter, make sure that it is read also in the church at Laodicea" (Colossians 4.16).

These different forms of writing, then – the Gospels, Luke's history of the Early Church which we call Acts, and letters from prominent church leaders – were eventually to come together to form the New Testament.

The Bible and us

The Bible is not just an ancient book of stories and theology. Everyday around the world, millions of Christians read the Bible and find it to be a source of guidance and practical help.

Where to find help when you are...

Afraid: Psalm 34.4–6; Isaiah 12.1–5; Matthew 10.28–31; 1 Peter 3.13–14

Angry: Matthew 5.22; Ephesians 4.25–27; James 1.19–20

Ashamed: Psalms 32; 51; Proverbs 17.9; Micah 7.18–20; Acts 13.38–39

Bitter : Psalms 73.21–26; Ephesians 4.31–32; James 3.13–18

Broke : Ecclesiastes 5.10–20; Matthew 6.24–34; 1 Timothy 6.6–10

Confused: Psalms 25.1–5; 32.8–9; Proverbs 3.1–6; Isaiah 42.16; Galatians 5.16–18

Depressed: Psalm 34; Isaiah 35.1–2

Discouraged: Psalms 41.5–11; 55.22; Matthew 5.11–12; 2 Corinthians 4.8–18; Philippians 4.4–7

Discriminated against: Acts 10.34–36; Galatians 3.26–29; Ephesians 2.11–22; 1 Corinthians 12.12–13

Doubting: Matthew 8.23–27; John 20.24–29; Jude verses 20–22

Feeling a failure: Psalms 136.1–19; Romans 8.31–39

Feeling let down by people: Luke 17.1–4; Romans 12.14–21

Feeling rejected: Psalms 86; 136; Romans 8.28, 38–39

Grieving: Psalm 147.2–3; Matthew 5.4; Revelation 21.3–4

Hating yourself: Psalm 139; 1 Corinthians 1:26–31; Colossians 3.12–13; 1 John 3.1–3

Impatient: Romans 12.11–12; Galatians 5.22–23; Hebrews 10.36

In need of protection: Numbers 6.22–26; Psalms 27.1–6,14; 56.8–13; 91; Nahum 1.7

Lonely: Psalms 22; 23; 40.1–3; 68.5–6

Needing peace: Luke 1.78–79; John 14.27–29; Romans 5.1–5; Philippians 4.6–7

Sad: Psalm 34.1–18; Isaiah 61.1–7; John 14.1; Revelation 21.3–4

Sick or in pain : Psalm 38; Proverbs 18.14; Matthew 14.34–36; James 5.14–15

Suffering: Psalm 102; 2 Corinthians 12.9–10; Colossians 1.24–2.5; 1 Peter 4.12–16,19

Tempted : Psalms 1; 139.23–24; 1 Corinthians 10.12–13; Hebrews 2.14–18; James 4.7; 2 Peter 3.17–18

Under pressure: Exodus 18.17–23; 1 Samuel 30.6; Job 19.1–27a; Psalm 43.1–4

Weary: Matthew 11.28–30; 1 Corinthians 15.58; Galatians 6.9–10

Worried: Psalms 46, 94.18–19; Matthew 6.19–34; John 14.27; Philippians 4.6; 1 Peter 5.6–7

Timeline

earliest times	Creation of the universe.
	Adam and Eve; Cain and Abel; Noah and the flood.
around 1900 BC	Abraham travels to Canaan.
around 1700 BC	The Israelites become slaves.
around 1600 BC	Jacob and family move to Egypt.
around 1290 BC	Exodus. Moses leads the Israelites out of Egypt.
	Institution of Passover.
around 1250 BC	Giving of the Law at Sinai.
	Israelites conquer Canaan.
around 1150–1050 BC	The time of the Judges.
1030–1010 BC	Reign of Saul.
1010–970 BC	Reign of David.
970–931 BC	Reign of Solomon.
931 BC	Kingdom splits into two: Judah in the south, Israel in the north.
around 870 BC	Time of Elijah.
around 850-800 BC	Time of Elisha.
around 750 BC	Time of prophets like Amos, Jonah, Hosea.
722 BC	Israel – the northern kingdom is destroyed by the Assyrians.
627 BC	Jeremiah begins his prophesying.
605 BC	Babylonians defeat the Egyptians to become the superpower in the Middle East.
around 600 BC	Babylonians invade Judah and deport some of the people, including Ezekiel and Daniel.
587 BC	Judah – the southern kingdom – is destroyed by the Babylonians.
	The people are taken into exile in Babylon.
539 BC	The first groups of exiles return to Jerusalem.
458/457 BC	Ezra returns to Jerusalem.
445 BC	Nehemiah returns to Jerusalem.
333 BC	Alexander the Great conquers the region including Judea.
around 167–163 BC	A revolt in Judea under the Maccabees brings independence.
63 BC	The Romans conquer the region.
around 5 BC	Birth of Jesus* and John the Baptist.
AD 33	Jesus' death and resurrection.
around AD 40	Church established in Antioch. Followers of Jesus first called Christians.
around AD 47-58	Paul's missionary journeys.
AD 58	Paul arrested in Jerusalem. Imprisoned in Caesarea.
AD 60	Paul goes to Rome.
around AD 92–96	On Patmos, John has a vision of present and future.

* When the Christian calendar was worked out in the sixth century, a mistake in working back to the date of Jesus' birth meant that it was a few years out.

The Old Testament

1 GENESIS

It's all about ... BEGINNINGS

The name *Genesis* means "origin" and that's what this book is all about: the creation of the universe, including the Earth and the entire human race. *Genesis* introduces many of the major themes of the Bible, such as sin, love, sacrifice and judgement. The book tells the stories of the ancestors of the Israelite nation — people like Adam, Noah, Abraham, Jacob and Joseph. These are known as "the patriarchs", which means "the fathers". God makes promises — known as "covenants" — to his people. These promises underpin God's relationship with his people throughout the rest of the Bible. God has promised to be with them — and he keeps his promises.

KEY EVENTS:
Creation (1–2); the sin of Adam and Eve (3); Noah and the ark (6–9); God's promises to Abraham (12–20); Jacob and Esau (25–27); Jacob's ladder (28); Jacob wrestles God (32); Joseph and his brothers (37–50).

The Story of Creation

1 **1** In the beginning, when God created the universe,* **2** the earth was formless and desolate. The raging ocean that covered everything was engulfed in total darkness, and the Spirit of God* was moving over the water. **3** *Then God commanded, "Let there be light" — and light appeared. **4** God was pleased with what he saw. Then he separated the light from the darkness, **5** and he named the light "Day"

and the darkness "Night". Evening passed and morning came — that was the first day.

6-7 *Then God commanded, "Let there be a dome to divide the water and to keep it in two separate places" — and it was done. So God made a dome, and it separated the water under it from the water above it. **8** He named the dome "Sky". Evening passed and morning came — that was the second day.

9 Then God commanded, "Let the water below the sky come together in one place, so that the land will appear" — and it was done. **10** He named the land "Earth", and the water which had come together he

---

1.1 *In the beginning… the universe;* or *In the beginning God created the universe;* or *When God began to create the universe.*

1.2 *the Spirit of God;* or *the power of God;* or *a wind from God;* or *an awesome wind.*

See also: 1.3: 2 Cor 4.6

See also: 1.6–8: 2 Pet 3.5

Let the earth produce all kinds of plants ... creatures that live in the water (1.11, 21)

named "Sea". And God was pleased with what he saw. **11** Then he commanded, "Let the earth produce all kinds of plants, those that bear grain and those that bear fruit" — and it was done. **12** So the earth produced all kinds of plants, and God was pleased with what he saw. **13** Evening passed and morning came — that was the third day.

14 Then God commanded, "Let lights appear in the sky to separate day from night and to show the time when days, years, and religious festivals* begin; **15** they will shine in the sky to give light to the earth" — and it was done. **16** So God made the two larger lights, the sun to rule over the day and the moon to rule over the night; he also made the stars. **17** He placed the lights in the sky to shine on the earth, **18** to rule over the day and the night, and to separate light from darkness. And God was pleased with what he saw. **19** Evening passed and morning came — that was the fourth day.

20 Then God commanded, "Let the water be filled with many kinds of living beings, and let the air be filled with birds." **21** So God created the great sea monsters, all kinds of creatures that live in the water, and all kinds of birds. And God was pleased with what he saw. **22** He blessed them all and told the creatures that live in the water to reproduce, and to fill the sea, and he told

Genesis 1

the birds to increase in number. **23** Evening passed and morning came — that was the fifth day.

24 Then God commanded, "Let the earth produce all kinds of animal life: domestic and wild, large and small" — and it was done. **25** So God made them all, and he was pleased with what he saw.

26 *Then God said, "And now we will make human beings; they will be like us and resemble us. They will have power over the fish, the birds, and all animals, domestic and wild,* large and small." **27** *So God created human beings, making them to be like himself. He created them male and female, **28** blessed them, and said, "Have many children, so that your descendants will live all over the earth and bring it under their control. I am putting you in charge of the fish, the birds, and all the wild animals. **29** I have provided all kinds of grain and all kinds of fruit for you to eat; **30** but for all the wild animals and for all the birds I have provided grass and leafy plants for food" — and it was done. **31** God looked at everything he had made, and he was very pleased. Evening passed and morning came — that was the sixth day.

2 **1** And so the whole universe was completed. **2** *By the seventh day God finished what he had been doing and stopped working. **3** He blessed the seventh day and set it apart as a special day, because by that day he had completed his creation* and stopped working. **4** And that is how the universe was created.

The Garden of Eden

When the LORD* God made the universe, **5** there were no plants on the earth and no seeds had sprouted, because he had not sent any rain, and there was no one to cultivate the land; **6** but water would come up from beneath the surface and water the ground.

....

1.26 One ancient translation *animals, domestic and wild;* Hebrew *domestic animals and all the earth.*
2.3 *by that day he had completed his creation;* or *on that day he completed his creation.*
2.4 *the LORD:* See LORD in Word List

See also: 1.26: 1 Cor 11.7   **1.27:** Mt 19.4;
Mk 10.6   **1.27–28:** Gen 5.1–2   **2.2:** Heb 4.4, 10
2.2–3: Ex 20.11

....

See also: 1.14 *religious festivals;* or *seasons.*

7 *Then the LORD God took some soil from the ground* and formed a man* out of it; he breathed life-giving breath into his nostrils and the man began to live.

8 Then the LORD God planted a garden in Eden, in the East, and there he put the man he had formed. **9** *He made all kinds of beautiful trees grow there and produce good fruit. In the middle of the garden stood the tree that gives life and the tree that gives knowledge of what is good and what is bad.*

10 A stream flowed in Eden and watered the garden; beyond Eden it divided into four rivers. **11** The first river is the Pishon; it flows round the country of Havilah. **12** (Pure gold is found there and also rare perfume and precious stones.) **13** The second river is the Gihon; it flows round the country of Cush.* **14** The third river is the Tigris, which flows east of Assyria, and the fourth river is the Euphrates.

15 Then the LORD God placed the man in the Garden of Eden to cultivate it and guard it. **16** He said to him, "You may eat the fruit of any tree in the garden, **17** except the tree that gives knowledge of what is good and what is bad.* You must not eat the fruit of that tree; if you do, you will die the same day."

18 Then the LORD God said, "It is not good for the man to live alone. I will make a suitable companion to help him." **19** So he took some soil from the ground and formed all the animals and all the birds. Then he brought them to the man to see what he would name them; and that is how they all got their names. **20** So the man named all the birds and all the animals; but not one of them was a suitable companion to help him.

21 Then the LORD God made the man fall into a deep sleep, and while he was sleeping, he took out one of the man's ribs and closed up the flesh. **22** He formed a woman out of the rib and brought her to him. **23** Then the man said,

"At last, here is one of my own kind —
Bone taken from my bone, and flesh from my flesh.
'Woman' is her name because she was taken out of man."*

24 *That is why a man leaves his father and mother and is united with his wife, and they become one.

25 The man and the woman were both naked, but they were not embarrassed.

Human Disobedience

3 **1** *Now the snake was the most cunning animal that the LORD God had made. The snake asked the woman, "Did God really tell you not to eat fruit from any tree in the garden?"

2 "We may eat the fruit of any tree in the garden," the woman answered, **3** "except the tree in the middle of it. God told us not to eat the fruit of that tree or even touch it; if we do, we will die."

4 The snake replied, "That's not true; you will not die. **5** God said that, because he knows that when you eat it you will be like God* and know what is good and what is bad."*

How wonderful it would be to become wise (3.6)

6 The woman saw how beautiful the tree was and how good its fruit would be to eat, and she thought how wonderful it would be to become wise. So she took some of the fruit and ate it. Then she gave some to

---

2.7 *ground... man:* The Hebrew words for "man" and "ground" have similar sounds.
2.9, 2.17 *knowledge of what is good and what is bad;* or *knowledge of everything.*
2.13 *Cush (of Mesopotamia);* or *Ethiopia.*

See also: 2.7: 1 Cor 15.45   **2.9:** Rev 2.7; 22.2, 14

2.23 *woman... man:* The Hebrew words for "woman" and "man" have similar sounds.
3.5 *God;* or *the gods.*
3.5 *know what is good and what is bad;* or *know everything.*

See also: 2.24: Mt 19.5; Mk 10.7–8; 1 Cor 6.16; Eph 5.31   **3.1:** Rev 12.9; 20.2

her husband, and he also ate it. **7** As soon as they had eaten it, they were given understanding and realized that they were naked; so they sewed fig leaves together and covered themselves.

8 That evening they heard the LORD God walking in the garden, and they hid from him among the trees. **9** But the LORD God called out to the man, "Where are you?"

10 He answered, "I heard you in the garden; I was afraid and hid from you, because I was naked."

11 "Who told you that you were naked?" God asked. "Did you eat the fruit that I told you not to eat?"

12 The man answered, "The woman you put here with me gave me the fruit, and I ate it."

13 *The LORD God asked the woman, "Why did you do this?"

She replied, "The snake tricked me into eating it."

God Pronounces Judgement

14 Then the LORD God said to the snake, "You will be punished for this; you alone of all the animals must bear this curse: from now on you will crawl on your belly, and you will have to eat dust as long as you live. **15** *I will make you and the woman hate each other; her offspring and yours will always be enemies. Her offspring will crush your head, and you will bite her offspring's* heel."

16 And he said to the woman, "I will increase your trouble in pregnancy and your pain in giving birth. In spite of this, you will still have desire for your husband, yet you will be subject to him."

17 *And he said to the man, "You listened to your wife and ate the fruit which I told you not to eat. Because of what you have done, the ground will be under a curse. You will have to work hard all your life to make it produce enough food for you. **18** It will produce weeds and thorns, and you will have to eat wild plants. **19** You will have to work hard and sweat to make the soil produce anything, until you go back to the soil from which you were formed. You were made from soil, and you will become soil again."

20 Adam* named his wife Eve,* because she was the mother of all human beings. **21** And the LORD God made clothes out of animal skins for Adam and his wife, and he clothed them.

Adam and Eve are Sent Out of the Garden

22 *Then the LORD God said, "Now the man has become like one of us and has knowledge of what is good and what is bad.* He must not be allowed to take fruit from the tree that gives life, eat it, and live for ever." **23** So the LORD God sent him out of the Garden of Eden and made him cultivate the soil from which he had been formed. **24** Then at the east side of the garden he put living creatures* and a flaming sword which turned in all directions. This was to keep anyone from coming near the tree that gives life.

Cain and Abel

4 **1** Then Adam had intercourse with his wife, and she became pregnant. She bore a son and said, "By the LORD's help I have acquired a son." So she named him Cain.* **2** Later she gave birth to another son, Abel. Abel became a shepherd, but Cain was a farmer. **3** After some time, Cain brought some of his harvest and gave it as an offering to the LORD. **4** *Then Abel brought the first lamb born to one of his sheep, killed it, and gave the best parts of it as an offering. The LORD was pleased with Abel and his offering, **5** but he rejected Cain and his offering. Cain became furious, and he scowled in anger. **6** Then the LORD said to Cain, "Why are you angry? Why that scowl on your face? **7** If you had done the right thing, you would be smiling;* but because you have done evil, sin is crouching at your door. It wants to rule you, but you must overcome it."

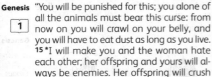

Genesis

1

3.15 *her offspring's*; or *their*.

See also: **3.13**: 2 Cor 11.3; 1 Tim 2.14
3.15: Rev 12.17   **3.17–18:** Heb 6.8

3.20 *Adam:* This name in Hebrew means "humanity".
3.20 *Eve:* This name sounds similar to the Hebrew word for "living", which is rendered in this context as "human beings".
3.22 *knowledge of what is good and what is bad;* or *knowledge of everything.*
3.24 *living creatures:* See Word List.
4.1 *Cain:* This name sounds like the Hebrew for "acquired".
4.7 *you would be smiling;* or *I would have accepted your offering.*

See also: **3.22:** Rev 22.14   **4.4:** Heb 11.4

Why that scowl on your face? (4.6)

16 And Cain went away from the LORD's presence and lived in a land called "Wandering", which is east of Eden.

The Descendants of Cain

17 Cain and his wife had a son and named him Enoch. Then Cain built a city and named it after his son. **18** Enoch had a son named Irad, who was the father of Mehujael, and Mehujael had a son named Methushael, who was the father of Lamech. **19** Lamech had two wives, Adah and Zillah. **20** Adah gave birth to Jabal, who was the ancestor of those who raise livestock and live in tents. **21** His brother was Jubal, the ancestor of all musicians who play the harp and the flute. **22** Zillah gave birth to Tubal Cain, who made all kinds of tools* out of bronze and iron. The sister of Tubal Cain was Naamah.

23 Lamech said to his wives,

"Adah and Zillah, listen to me: I have
    killed a young man because he
    struck me.

24 *If seven lives are taken to pay for
    killing Cain,
77 will be taken if anyone kills me."

Seth and Enosh

25 Adam and his wife had another son. She said, "God has given me a son to replace Abel, whom Cain killed." So she named him Seth.* **26** Seth had a son whom he named Enosh. It was then that people began using the LORD's holy name in worship.

The Descendants of Adam
(1 Chr 1.1–4)

5 **1** *This is the list of the descendants of Adam. (When God created human beings, he made them like himself. **2** *He created them male and female, blessed them, and named them "Humanity".) **3** When Adam was 130 years old, he had a son who was like him, and he named him Seth. **4** After that, Adam lived another 800 years. He had other children **5** and died at the age of 930.

8 *Then Cain said to his brother Abel, "Let's go out in the fields."* When they were out in the fields, Cain turned on his brother and killed him.

9 The LORD asked Cain, "Where is your brother Abel?"

He answered, "I don't know. Am I supposed to take care of my brother?"

10 *Then the LORD said, "Why have you done this terrible thing? Your brother's blood is crying out to me from the ground, like a voice calling for revenge. **11** You are placed under a curse and can no longer farm the soil. It has soaked up your brother's blood as if it had opened its mouth to receive it when you killed him. **12** If you try to grow crops, the soil will not produce anything; you will be a homeless wanderer on the earth."

13 And Cain said to the LORD, "This punishment is too hard for me to bear. **14** You are driving me off the land and away from your presence. I will be a homeless wanderer on the earth, and anyone who finds me will kill me."

15 But the LORD answered, "No. If anyone kills you, seven lives will be taken in revenge." So the LORD put a mark on Cain to warn anyone who met him not to kill him.

4.8 Some ancient translations *Let's go out in the fields;* Hebrew does not have these words.

4.22 *who made all kinds of tools;* one ancient translation *ancestor of all metalworkers.*
4.25 *Seth:* This name sounds like the Hebrew for "has given".

See also: 4.8: Mt 23.35; Lk 11.51; 1 Jn 3.12
4.10: Heb 12.24

See also: 4.24: Mt 18.22   **5.1–2:** Gen 1.27–28
5.2: Mt 19.4; Mk 10.6

6 When Seth was 105, he had a son, Enosh, **7** and then lived another 807 years. He had other children **8** and died at the age of 912.

9 When Enosh was ninety, he had a son, Kenan, **10** and then lived another 815 years. He had other children **11** and died at the age of 905.

12 When Kenan was seventy, he had a son, Mahalalel, **13** and then lived another 840 years. He had other children **14** and died at the age of 910.

15 When Mahalalel was 65, he had a son, Jared, **16** and then lived another 830 years. He had other children **17** and died at the age of 895.

18 When Jared was 162, he had a son, Enoch, **19** and then lived another 800 years. He had other children **20** and died at the age of 962.

21 When Enoch was 65, he had a son, Methuselah. **22** After that, Enoch lived in fellowship with God for 300 years and had other children. **23** He lived to be 365 years old. **24** *He spent his life in fellowship with God, and then he disappeared, because God took him away.

Genesis
1

25 When Methuselah was 187, he had a son, Lamech, **26** and then lived another 782 years. He had other children **27** and died at the age of 969.

28 When Lamech was 182, he had a son, **29** and said, "From the very ground on which the LORD put a curse, this child will bring us relief from all our hard work"; so he named him Noah.* **30** Lamech lived another 595 years. He had other children **31** and died at the age of 777.

32 After Noah was 500 years old, he had three sons, Shem, Ham, and Japheth.

Human Wickedness

6 **1** *When the human race had spread all over the world, and daughters were being born, **2** some of the heavenly beings* saw that these young women were beautiful, so they took the ones they liked. **3** Then the LORD said, "I will not allow people to live for ever; they are mortal. From now on they

will live no longer than 120 years." **4** *In those days, and even later, there were giants on the earth who were descendants of human women and the heavenly beings.* They were the great heroes and famous men of long ago.

5 *When the LORD saw how wicked everyone on earth was and how evil their thoughts were all the time, **6** he was sorry that he had ever made them and put them on the earth. He was so filled with regret **7** that he said, "I will wipe out these people I have created, and also the animals and the birds, because I am sorry that I made any of them." **8** But the LORD was pleased with Noah.

Noah

9-10 *This is the story of Noah. He had three sons, Shem, Ham, and Japheth. Noah had no faults and was the only good man of his time. He lived in fellowship with God, **11** but everyone else was evil in God's sight, and violence had spread everywhere. **12** God looked at the world and saw that it was evil, for the people were all living evil lives.

13 God said to Noah, "I have decided to put an end to the whole human race. I will destroy them completely, because the world is full of their violent deeds. **14** Build a boat for yourself out of good timber; make rooms in it and cover it with tar inside and out. **15** Make it 133 metres long, 22 metres wide, and thirteen metres high. **16** Make a roof* for the boat and leave a space of 44 centimetres between the roof* and the sides. Build it with three decks and put a door in the side. **17** I am going to send a flood on the earth to destroy every living being. Everything on the earth will die, **18** but I will make a covenant with you. Go into the boat with your wife, your sons, and their wives. **19-20** Take into the boat with you a male and a female of every kind of animal and of every kind of bird, in order to keep them alive. **21** Take along all kinds of food for you and for them." **22** *Noah did everything that God commanded.

....

5.29 *Noah:* This name sounds like the Hebrew for "relief".
6.2, 6.4 *heavenly beings;* or *sons of the gods;* or *sons of God.*

See also: 5.24: Heb 11.5; Jude 14   **6.1–4:** Job 1.6; 2.1

....

6.4, 6.2 *heavenly beings;* or *sons of the gods;* or *sons of God.*
6.16 *roof;* or *window.*

See also: 6.4: Num 13.33   **6.5–8:** Mt 24.37; Lk 17.26; 1 Pet 3.20   **6.9:** 2 Pet 2.5   **6.22:** Heb 11.7

Every kind of animal and bird … went into the boat (7.8, 9)

The Flood

7 **1** The LORD said to Noah, "Go into the boat with your whole family; I have found that you are the only one in all the world who does what is right. **2** Take with you seven pairs of each kind of ritually clean animal, but only one pair of each kind of unclean animal. **3** Take also seven pairs of each kind of bird. Do this so that every kind of animal and bird will be kept alive to reproduce again on the earth. **4** Seven days from now I am going to send rain that will fall for forty days and nights, in order to destroy all the living beings that I have made." **5** And Noah did everything that the LORD commanded.

6 Noah was 600 years old when the flood came on the earth. **7** *He and his wife, and his sons and their wives, went into the boat to escape the flood. **8** A male and a female of every kind of animal and bird, whether ritually clean or unclean, **9** went into the boat with Noah, as God had commanded. **10** Seven days later the flood came.

11 *When Noah was 600 years old, on the seventeenth day of the second month all the outlets of the vast body of water beneath the earth burst open, all the floodgates of the sky were opened, **12** and rain fell on the earth for forty days and nights. **13** On that same day Noah and his wife went into the boat with their three sons, Shem, Ham, and Japheth, and their wives.

14 With them went every kind of animal, domestic and wild, large and small, and every kind of bird. **15** A male and a female of each kind of living being went into the boat with Noah, **16** as God had commanded. Then the LORD shut the door behind Noah.

17 The flood continued for forty days, and the water became deep enough for the boat to float. **18** The water became deeper, and the boat drifted on the surface. **19** It became so deep that it covered the highest mountains; **20** it went on rising until it was about seven metres above the tops of the mountains. **21** Every living being on the earth died — every bird, every animal, and every person. **22** Everything on earth that breathed died. **23** The LORD destroyed all living beings on the earth — human beings, animals, and birds. The only ones left

Everything on earth that breathed died (7.22)

See also: 7.7: Mt 24.38–39; Lk 17.27　**7.11:** 2 Pet 3.6

were Noah and those who were with him in the boat. **24** The water did not start going down for 150 days.

The End of the Flood

8 **1** God had not forgotten Noah and all the animals with him in the boat; he caused a wind to blow, and the water started going down. **2** The outlets of the water beneath the earth and the floodgates of the sky were closed. The rain stopped, **3** and the water gradually went down for 150 days. **4** On the seventeenth day of the seventh month the boat came to rest on a mountain in the Ararat range. **5** The water kept going down, and on the first day of the tenth month the tops of the mountains appeared.

Genesis

1

So Noah knew that the water had gone down (8.11)

6 After forty days Noah opened a window **7** and sent out a raven. It did not come back, but kept flying around until the water was completely gone. **8** Meanwhile, Noah sent out a dove to see if the water had gone down, **9** but since the water still covered all the land, the dove did not find a place to alight. It flew back to the boat, and Noah reached out and took it in. **10** He waited another seven days and sent out the dove again. **11** It returned to him in the evening with a fresh olive leaf in its beak. So Noah knew that the water had gone down. **12** Then he waited another seven days and sent out the dove once more; this time it did not come back.

13 When Noah was 601 years old, on the first day of the first month, the water was gone. Noah removed the covering of the boat, looked round, and saw that the ground was getting dry. **14** By the 27th day of the second month the earth was completely dry.

15 God said to Noah, **16** "Go out of the boat with your wife, your sons, and their wives. **17** Take all the birds and animals out with you, so that they may reproduce and spread over all the earth." **18** So Noah went out of the boat with his wife, his sons, and their wives. **19** All the animals and birds went out of the boat in groups of their own kind.

Noah Offers a Sacrifice

20 Noah built an altar to the LORD; he took one of each kind of ritually clean animal and bird, and burnt them whole as a sacrifice on the altar. **21** The odour of the sacrifice pleased the LORD, and he said to himself, "Never again will I put the earth under a curse because of what people do; I know that from the time they are young their thoughts are evil. Never again will I destroy all living beings, as I have done this time. **22** As long as the world exists, there will be a time for planting and a time for harvest. There will always be cold and heat, summer and winter, day and night."

God's Covenant with Noah

9 **1** *God blessed Noah and his sons and said, "Have many children, so that your descendants will live all over the earth. **2** All the animals, birds, and fish will live in fear of you. They are all placed under your power. **3** Now you can eat them, as well as green plants; I give them all to you for food. **4** *The one thing you must not eat is meat with blood still in it; I forbid this because the life is in the blood. **5** If anyone takes human life, he will be punished. I will punish with death any animal that takes a human life. **6** *Human beings were made like God, so whoever murders one of them will be killed by someone else.

7 *"You must have many children, so that your descendants will live all over the earth."

8 God said to Noah and his sons, **9** "I am now making my covenant with you and with your descendants, **10** and with all living beings — all birds and all animals — everything that came out of the boat with you. **11** With these words I make my

See also: 9.1: Gen 1.28   **9.4:** Lev 7.26–27; 17.10–14; 19.26; Deut 12.16, 23; 15.23   **9.6:** Gen 1.26; Ex 20.13   **9.7:** Gen 1.28

covenant with you: I promise that never again will all living beings be destroyed by a flood; never again will a flood destroy the earth. **12** As a sign of this everlasting covenant which I am making with you and with all living beings, I am putting my bow in the clouds. It will be the sign of my covenant with the world. **14** Whenever I cover the sky with clouds and the rainbow appears, **15** I will remember my promise to you and to all the animals that a flood will never again destroy all living beings. **16** When the rainbow appears in the clouds, I will see it and remember the everlasting covenant between me and all living beings on earth. **17** That is the sign of the promise which I am making to all living beings."

The sign of my covenant with the world (9.13)

Noah and his Sons

18 The sons of Noah who went out of the boat were Shem, Ham, and Japheth. (Ham was the father of Canaan.) **19** These three sons of Noah were the ancestors of all the people on earth.

20 Noah, who was a farmer, was the first man to plant a vineyard. **21** After he drank some of the wine, he became drunk, took off his clothes, and lay naked in his tent. **22** When Ham, the father of Canaan, saw that his father was naked, he went out and told his two brothers. **23** Then Shem and Japheth took a robe and held it behind them on their shoulders. They walked backwards into the tent and covered their father, keeping their faces turned away so as not to see him naked. **24** When Noah was sober again and learnt what his youngest son had done to him, **25** he said,

"A curse on Canaan!

He will be a slave to his brothers.

26 Give praise to the LORD, the God of Shem!

Canaan will be the slave of Shem.

27 May God cause Japheth* to increase!

May his descendants live with the people of Shem!

Canaan will be the slave of Japheth."

28 After the flood Noah lived for 350 years **29** and died at the age of 950.

The Descendants of Noah's Sons
(1 Chr 1.5–23)

10 **1** These are the descendants of Noah's sons, Shem, Ham, and Japheth. These three had sons after the flood.

2 The sons of Japheth — Gomer, Magog, Madai, Javan, Tubal, Meshech, and Tiras — were the ancestors of the peoples who bear their names. **3** The descendants of Gomer were the people of Ashkenaz, Riphath, and Togarmah. **4** The descendants of Javan were the people of Elishah, Spain, Cyprus, and Rhodes; **5** they were the ancestors of the people who live along the coast and on the islands. These are the descendants of Japheth, living in their different tribes and countries, each group speaking its own language.

6 The sons of Ham — Cush, Egypt, Libya and Canaan — were the ancestors of the peoples who bear their names. **7** The descendants of Cush were the people of Seba, Havilah, Sabtah, Raamah, and Sabteca. The descendants of Raamah were the people of Sheba and Dedan. **8** Cush had a son named Nimrod, who became the world's first great conqueror. **9** By the LORD's help he was a great hunter, and that is why people say, "May the LORD make you as great a hunter as Nimrod!" **10** At first his kingdom included Babylon, Erech, and Accad, all three of them in Babylonia. **11** From that land he went to Assyria and built the cities of Nineveh, Rehoboth Ir, Calah, **12** and Resen, which is between Nineveh and the great city of Calah.

13 The descendants of Egypt were the people of Lydia, Anam, Lehab, Naphtuh, **14** Pathrus, Casluh, and of Crete, from whom the Philistines are descended.*

9.27 *Japheth:* This name sounds like the Hebrew for "increase".

10.14 Probable text *and of Crete… descended;* Hebrew *from whom the Philistines are descended, and Crete.*

15 Canaan's sons — Sidon, the eldest, and Heth — were the ancestors of the peoples who bear their names. **16** Canaan was also the ancestor of the Jebusites, the Amorites, the Girgashites, **17** the Hivites, the Arkites, the Sinites, **18** the Arvadites, the Zemarites, and the Hamathites. The different tribes of the Canaanites spread out, **19** until the Canaanite borders reached from Sidon southwards to Gerar near Gaza, and eastwards to Sodom, Gomorrah, Admah, and Zeboiim near Lasha. **20** These are the descendants of Ham, living in their different tribes and countries, each group speaking its own language.

21 Shem, the elder brother of Japheth, was the ancestor of all the Hebrews. **22** Shem's sons — Elam, Asshur, Arpachshad, Lud, and Aram — were the ancestors of the peoples who bear their names. **23** The descendants of Aram were the people of Uz, Hul, Gether, and Meshek. **24** Arpachshad was the father of Shelah, who was the father of Eber. **25** Eber had two sons: one was named Peleg,* because during his time the people of the world were divided; and the other was named Joktan. **26** The descendants of Joktan were the people of Almodad, Sheleph, Hazarmaveth, Jerah, **27** Hadoram, Uzal, Diklah, **28** Obal, Abimael, Sheba, **29** Ophir, Havilah, and Jobab. All of them were descended from Joktan. **30** The land in which they lived extended from Mesha to Sephar in the eastern hill country. **31** These are the descendants of Shem, living in their different tribes and countries, each group speaking its own language.

32 All these peoples are the descendants of Noah, nation by nation, according to their different lines of descent. After the flood all the nations of the earth were descended from the sons of Noah.

Genesis

[1]

The Tower of Babylon

11 **1** At first, the people of the whole world had only one language and used the same words. **2** As they wandered about in the East, they came to a plain in Babylonia and settled there. **3** They said to one another, "Come on! Let's make bricks and bake them hard." So they had bricks

to build with and tar to hold them together. **4** They said, "Now let's build a city with a tower that reaches the sky, so that we can make a name for ourselves and not be scattered all over the earth."

5 Then the LORD came down to see the city and the tower which those men had built, **6** and he said, "Now then, these are all one people and they speak one language; this is just the beginning of what they are going to do. Soon they will be able to do anything they want! **7** Let us go down and mix up their language so that they will not understand one another." **8** So the LORD scattered them all over the earth, and they stopped building the city. **9** The city was called Babylon,* because there the LORD mixed up the language of all the people, and from there he scattered them all over the earth.

The Descendants of Shem
(1 Chr 1.24–27)

10 These are the descendants of Shem. Two years after the flood, when Shem was 100 years old, he had a son, Arpachshad. **11** After that, he lived another 500 years and had other children.

12 When Arpachshad was 35 years old, he had a son, Shelah; **13** after that, he lived another 403 years and had other children.

14 When Shelah was thirty years old, he had a son, Eber; **15** after that, he lived another 403 years and had other children.

16 When Eber was 34 years old, he had a son, Peleg; **17** after that, he lived another 430 years and had other children.

18 When Peleg was thirty years old, he had a son, Reu; **19** after that, he lived another 209 years and had other children.

20 When Reu was 32 years old, he had a son, Serug; **21** after that, he lived another 207 years and had other children.

22 When Serug was thirty years old, he had a son, Nahor; **23** after that, he lived another 200 years and had other children.

24 When Nahor was 29 years old, he had a son, Terah; **25** after that, he lived another 119 years and had other children.

26 After Terah was seventy years old, he became the father of Abram, Nahor, and Haran.

10.25 *Peleg:* This name sounds like the Hebrew for "divide".

11.9 *Babylon:* This name sounds like the Hebrew for "mixed up".

The Descendants of Terah

27 These are the descendants of Terah, who was the father of Abram, Nahor, and Haran. Haran was the father of Lot, **28** and Haran died in his native city, Ur in Babylonia, while his father was still living. **29** Abram married Sarai, and Nahor married Milcah, the daughter of Haran, who was also the father of Iscah. **30** Sarai was not able to have children.

31 Terah took his son Abram, his grandson Lot, who was the son of Haran, and his daughter-in-law Sarai, Abram's wife, and with them he left the city of Ur in Babylonia to go to the land of Canaan. They went as far as Haran and settled there. **32** Terah died there at the age of 205.

God's Call to Abram

12 **1** *The LORD said to Abram, "Leave your country, your relatives, and your father's home, and go to a land that I am going to show you. **2** I will give you many descendants, and they will become a great nation. I will bless you and make your name famous, so that you will be a blessing.

3 *I will bless those who bless you,
But I will curse those who curse you.
And through you I will bless all the nations."*

4 When Abram was 75 years old, he started out from Haran, as the LORD had told him to do; and Lot went with him. **5** Abram took his wife Sarai, his nephew Lot, and all the wealth and all the slaves they had acquired in Haran, and they started out for the land of Canaan.

When they arrived in Canaan, **6** Abram travelled through the land until he came to the sacred tree of Moreh, the holy place at Shechem. (At that time the Canaanites were still living in the land.) **7** *The LORD appeared to Abram and said to him, "This is the country that I am going to give to your descendants." Then Abram built an altar there to the LORD, who had appeared to him. **8** After that, he moved on south to the hill country east of the city of Bethel and set up his camp between Bethel on the

west and Ai on the east. There also he built an altar and worshipped the LORD. **9** Then he moved on from place to place, going towards the southern part of Canaan.

Abram in Egypt

10 But there was a famine in Canaan, and it was so bad that Abram went farther south to Egypt, to live there for a while. **11** When he was about to cross the border into Egypt, he said to his wife Sarai, "You are a beautiful woman. **12** When the Egyptians see you, they will assume that you are my wife, and so they will kill me and let you live. **13** *Tell them that you are my sister; then because of you they will let me live and treat me well." **14** When he crossed the border into Egypt, the Egyptians did see that his wife was beautiful. **15** Some of the court officials saw her and told the king how beautiful she was; so she was taken to his palace. **16** Because of her the king treated Abram well and gave him flocks of sheep and goats, cattle, donkeys, slaves, and camels.

17 But because the king had taken Sarai, the LORD sent terrible diseases on him and on the people of his palace. **18** Then the king sent for Abram and asked him, "What have you done to me? Why didn't you tell me that she was your wife? **19** Why did you say that she was your sister, and let me take her as my wife? Here is your wife; take her and get out!" **20** The king gave orders to his men, so they took Abram and put him out of the country, together with his wife and everything he owned.

Abram and Lot Separate

13 **1** Abram went north out of Egypt to the southern part of Canaan with his wife and everything he owned, and Lot went with him. **2** Abram was a very rich man, with sheep, goats, and cattle, as well as silver and gold. **3** Then he left there and moved from place to place, going towards Bethel. He reached the place between Bethel and Ai where he had camped before **4** and had built an altar. There he worshipped the LORD.

5 Lot also had sheep, goats, and cattle, as well as his own family and servants. **6** And so there was not enough pasture land for

12.3 *And through… nations;* or *All the nations will ask me to bless them as I have blessed you.*

See also: 12.1: Acts 7.2–3; Heb 11.8　　**12.3:** Gal 3.8
12.7: Acts 7.5; Gal 3.16

See also: 12.13: Gen 20.2; 26.7

the two of them to stay together, because they had too many animals. **7** So quarrels broke out between the men who took care of Abram's animals and those who took care of Lot's animals. (At that time the Canaanites and the Perizzites were still living in the land.)

8 Then Abram said to Lot, "We are relatives, and your men and my men shouldn't be quarrelling. **9** So let's separate. Choose any part of the land you want. You go one way, and I'll go the other."

10 *Lot looked round and saw that the whole Jordan Valley, all the way to Zoar, had plenty of water, like the Garden of the LORD* or like the land of Egypt. (This was before the LORD had destroyed the cities of Sodom and Gomorrah.) **11** So Lot chose the whole Jordan Valley for himself and moved away towards the east. That is how the two men parted. **12** Abram stayed in the land of Canaan, and Lot settled among the cities in the valley and camped near Sodom, **13** whose people were wicked and sinned against the LORD.

Genesis

1

Abram Moves to Hebron

14 After Lot had left, the LORD said to Abram, "From where you are, look carefully in all directions. **15** *I am going to give you and your descendants all the land that you see, and it will be yours for ever. **16** I am going to give you so many descendants that no one will be able to count them all; it would be as easy to count all the specks of dust on earth! **17** Now, go and look over the whole land, because I am going to give it all to you." **18** So Abram moved his camp and settled near the sacred trees of Mamre at Hebron, and there he built an altar to the LORD.

Abram Rescues Lot

14 **1** Four kings, Amraphel of Babylonia, Arioch of Ellasar, Chedorlaomer of Elam, and Tidal of Goiim, **2** went to war against five other kings: Bera of Sodom, Birsha of Gomorrah, Shinab of Admah, Shemeber of Zeboiim, and the king of Bela (or Zoar). **3** These five kings had formed an alliance and joined forces in the Valley

of Siddim, which is now the Dead Sea. **4** They had been under the control of Chedorlaomer for twelve years, but in the thirteenth year they rebelled against him. **5** In the fourteenth year Chedorlaomer and his allies came with their armies and defeated the Rephaim in Ashteroth Karnaim, the Zuzim in Ham, the Emim in the plain of Kiriathaim, **6** and the Horites in the mountains of Edom, pursuing them as far as Elparan on the edge of the desert. **7** Then they turned round and came back to Kadesh (then known as Enmishpat). They conquered all the land of the Amalekites and defeated the Amorites who lived in Hazazon Tamar.

8 Then the kings of Sodom, Gomorrah, Admah, Zeboiim, and Bela drew up their armies for battle in the Valley of Siddim and fought **9** against the kings of Elam, Goiim, Babylonia, and Ellasar, five kings against four. **10** The valley was full of tar pits, and when the kings of Sodom and Gomorrah tried to run away from the battle, they fell into the pits; but the other three kings escaped to the mountains. **11** The four kings took everything in Sodom and Gomorrah, including the food, and went away. **12** Lot, Abram's nephew, was living in Sodom, so they took him and all his possessions.

13 But a man escaped and reported all this to Abram, the Hebrew, who was living near the sacred trees belonging to Mamre the Amorite. Mamre and his brothers Eshcol and Aner were Abram's allies. **14** When Abram heard that his nephew had been captured, he called together all the fighting men in his camp, 318 in all, and pursued the four kings all the way to Dan. **15** There he divided his men into groups, attacked the enemy by night, and defeated them. He chased them as far as Hobah, north of Damascus, **16** and recovered the loot that had been taken. He also brought back his nephew Lot and his possessions, together with the women and the other prisoners.

Melchizedek Blesses Abram

17 When Abram came back from his victory over Chedorlaomer and the other kings, the king of Sodom went out to meet him in the Valley of Shaveh (also called the King's Valley). **18** *And Melchizedek, who was king of Salem and also a priest of the

---

13.10 *Garden of the LORD:* a reference to the Garden of Eden.

See also: 13.10: Gen 2.10   **13.15:** Acts 7.5

See also: 14.18–20: Heb 7.1–10

Most High God, brought bread and wine to Abram, **19** blessed him, and said, "May the Most High God, who made heaven and earth, bless Abram! **20** May the Most High God, who gave you victory over your enemies, be praised!" And Abram gave Melchizedek a tenth of all the loot he had recovered.

21 The king of Sodom said to Abram, "Keep the loot, but give me back all my people."

22 Abram answered, "I solemnly swear before the LORD, the Most High God, Maker of heaven and earth, **23** that I will not keep anything of yours, not even a thread or a sandal strap. Then you can never say, 'I am the one who made Abram rich.' **24** I will take nothing for myself. I will accept only what my men have used. But let my allies, Aner, Eshcol, and Mamre, take their share."

God's Covenant with Abram

15 **1** After this, Abram had a vision and heard the LORD say to him, "Do not be afraid, Abram. I will shield you from danger and give you a great reward."

2 But Abram answered, "Sovereign LORD, what good will your reward do me, since I have no children? My only heir is Eliezer of Damascus.* **3** You have given me no children, and one of my slaves will inherit my property."

4 Then he heard the LORD speaking to him again: "This slave Eliezer will not inherit your property; your own son will be your heir." **5** *The LORD took him outside and said, "Look at the sky and try to count the stars; you will have as many descendants as that."

6 *Abram put his trust in the LORD, and because of this the LORD was pleased with him and accepted him.

7 Then the LORD said to him, "I am the LORD, who led you out of Ur in Babylonia, to give you this land as your own."

8 But Abram asked, "Sovereign LORD, how can I know that it will be mine?"

9 He answered, "Bring me a cow, a goat, and a ram, each of them three years old, and a dove and a pigeon." **10** Abram brought the animals to God, cut them in half, and placed the halves opposite each other in two rows; but he did not cut up the birds. **11** Vultures came down on the bodies, but Abram drove them off.

12 *When the sun was going down, Abram fell into a deep sleep, and fear and terror came over him. **13** *The LORD said to him, "Your descendants will be strangers in a foreign land; they will be slaves there and will be treated cruelly for 400 years. **14** *But I will punish the nation that enslaves them, and when they leave that foreign land, they will take great wealth with them. **15** You yourself will live to a ripe old age, die in peace, and be buried. **16** It will be four generations before your descendants come back here, because I will not drive out the Amorites until they become so wicked that they must be punished."

17 When the sun had set and it was dark, a smoking fire-pot and a flaming torch suddenly appeared and passed between the pieces of the animals. **18** *Then and there the LORD made a covenant with Abram. He said, "I promise to give your descendants all this land from the border of Egypt to the River Euphrates, **19** including the lands of the Kenites, the Kenizzites, the Kadmonites, **20** the Hittites, the Perizzites, the Rephaim, **21** the Amorites, the Canaanites, the Girgashites, and the Jebusites."

Hagar and Ishmael

16 **1** Abram's wife Sarai had not borne him any children. But she had an Egyptian slave woman named Hagar, **2** and so she said to Abram, "The LORD has kept me from having children. Why don't you sleep with my slave? Perhaps she can have a child for me." Abram agreed with what Sarai said. **3** So she gave Hagar to him to be his concubine. (This happened after Abram had lived in Canaan for ten years.) **4** Abram had intercourse with Hagar, and she became pregnant. When she found out that she was pregnant, she became proud and despised Sarai.

5 Then Sarai said to Abram, "It's your fault that Hagar despises me.* I myself

---

15.2 *My... Damascus;* Hebrew unclear.

See also: 15.5: Rom 4.18; Heb 11.12
15.6: Rom 4.3; Gal 3.6; Jas 2.23

16.5 *It's your fault... me;* or *May you suffer for this wrong done against me.*

See also: 15.12: Job 4.13, 14   **15.13:** Ex 1.1–14; Acts 7.6   **15.14:** Ex 12.40–41; Acts 7.7
15.18: Acts 7.5

gave her to you, and ever since she found out that she was pregnant, she has despised me. May the LORD judge which of us is right, you or me!"

6 Abram answered, "Very well, she is your slave and under your control; do whatever you want with her." Then Sarai treated Hagar so cruelly that she ran away.

7 The angel of the LORD met Hagar at a spring in the desert on the road to Shur **8** and said, "Hagar, slave of Sarai, where have you come from and where are you going?"

She answered, "I am running away from my mistress."

9 He said, "Go back to her and be her slave." **10** Then he said, "I will give you so many descendants that no one will be able to count them. **11** You are going to have a son, and you will name him Ishmael,* because the LORD has heard your cry of distress. **12** But your son will live like a wild donkey; he will be against everyone, and everyone will be against him. He will live apart from all his relatives."

13 Hagar asked herself, "Have I really seen God and lived to tell about it?"* So she called the LORD who had spoken to her "A God who Sees". **14** That is why people call the well between Kadesh and Bered "The Well of the Living One who Sees Me".

15 *Hagar bore Abram a son, and he named him Ishmael. **16** Abram was 86 years old at the time.

Circumcision, the Sign of the Covenant

17 **1** When Abram was 99 years old, the LORD appeared to him and said, "I am the Almighty God. Obey me and always do what is right. **2** I will make my covenant with you and give you many descendants." **3** Abram bowed down with his face touching the ground, and God said, **4** "I make this covenant with you: I promise that you will be the ancestor of many nations. **5** *Your name will no longer be Abram, but Abraham,* because I am

making you the ancestor of many nations. **6** I will give you many descendants, and some of them will be kings. You will have so many descendants that they will become nations.

7 *"I will keep my promise to you and to your descendants in future generations as an everlasting covenant. I will be your God and the God of your descendants. **8** *I will give to you and to your descendants this land in which you are now a foreigner. The whole land of Canaan will belong to your descendants for ever, and I will be their God."

9 God said to Abraham, "You also must agree to keep the covenant with me, both you and your descendants in future generations. **10** *You and your descendants must all agree to circumcise every male among you. **11-12** From now on you must circumcise every baby boy when he is eight days old, including slaves born in your homes and slaves bought from foreigners. This will show that there is a covenant between you and me. **13** Each one must be circumcised, and this will be a physical sign to show that my covenant with you is everlasting. **14** Any male who has not been circumcised will no longer be considered one of my people, because he has not kept the covenant with me."

15 God said to Abraham, "You must no longer call your wife Sarai; from now on her name is Sarah.* **16** I will bless her, and I will give you a son by her. I will bless her, and she will become the mother of nations, and there will be kings among her descendants."

17 Abraham bowed down with his face touching the ground, but he began to laugh when he thought, "Can a man have a child when he is a hundred years old? Can Sarah have a child at ninety?" **18** He asked God, "Why not let Ishmael be my heir?"

19 But God said, "No. Your wife Sarah will bear you a son and you will name him Isaac.* I will keep my covenant with him and with his descendants for ever. It is an everlasting covenant. **20** I have heard your request about Ishmael, so I will bless him

---

16.11 *Ishmael:* This name in Hebrew means "God hears".

16.13 Probable text *lived to tell about it?*; Hebrew unclear.

17.5 *Abraham:* This name sounds like the Hebrew for "ancestor of many nations".

See also: 16.15: Gal 4.22   **17.5:** Rom 4.17

17.15 *Sarah:* This name in Hebrew means "princess".

17.19 *Isaac:* This name in Hebrew means "he laughs".

See also: 17.7: Lk 1.55   **17.8:** Acts 7.5

17.10: Acts 7.8; Rom 4.11

and give him many children and many descendants. He will be the father of twelve princes, and I will make a great nation of his descendants. **21** But I will keep my covenant with your son Isaac, who will be born to Sarah about this time next year." **22** When God finished speaking to Abraham, he left him.

23 On that same day Abraham obeyed God and circumcised his son Ishmael and all the other males in his household, including the slaves born in his home and those he had bought. **24** Abraham was 99 years old when he was circumcised, **25** and his son Ishmael was thirteen. **26** They were both circumcised on the same day, **27** together with all Abraham's slaves.

A Son is Promised to Abraham

18 **1** The LORD appeared to Abraham at the sacred trees of Mamre. As Abraham was sitting at the entrance of his tent during the hottest part of the day, **2** *he looked up and saw three men standing there. As soon as he saw them, he ran out to meet them. Bowing down with his face touching the ground, **3** he said, "Sirs, please do not pass by my home without stopping; I am here to serve you. **4** Let me bring some water for you to wash your feet; you can rest here beneath this tree. **5** I will also bring a bit of food; it will give you strength to continue your journey. You have honoured me by coming to my home, so let me serve you."

They replied, "Thank you; we accept."

6 Abraham hurried into the tent and said to Sarah, "Quick, take a sack of your best flour, and bake some bread." **7** Then he ran to the herd and picked out a calf that was tender and fat, and gave it to a servant, who hurried to get it ready. **8** He took some cream, some milk, and the meat, and set the food before the men. There under the tree he served them himself, and they ate.

9 Then they asked him, "Where is your wife Sarah?"

"She is there in the tent," he answered.

10 *One of them said, "Nine months from now* I will come back, and your wife Sarah will have a son."

Sarah was behind him, at the door of the tent, listening. **11** Abraham and Sarah were very old, and Sarah had stopped having her monthly periods. **12** *So Sarah laughed to herself and said, "Now that I am old and worn out, can I still enjoy sex? And besides, my husband is old too."

13 Then the LORD asked Abraham, "Why did Sarah laugh and say, 'Can I really have a child when I am so old?' **14** *Is anything too hard for the LORD? As I said, nine months from now I will return, and Sarah will have a son."

15 Because Sarah was afraid, she denied it. "I didn't laugh," she said.

"Yes, you did," he replied. "You laughed."

Abraham Pleads for Sodom

16 Then the men left and went to a place where they could look down at Sodom, and Abraham went with them to send them on their way. **17** And the LORD said to himself, "I will not hide from Abraham what I am going to do. **18** His descendants will become a great and mighty nation, and through him I will bless all the nations.* **19** I have chosen him in order that he may command his sons and his descendants to obey me and to do what is right and just. If they do, I will do everything for him that I have promised."

20 Then the LORD said to Abraham, "There are terrible accusations against Sodom and Gomorrah, and their sin is very great. **21** I must go down to find out whether or not the accusations which I have heard are true."

22 Then the two men left and went on towards Sodom, but the LORD remained with Abraham. **23** Abraham approached the LORD and asked, "Are you really going to destroy the innocent with the guilty? **24** If there are fifty innocent people in the city, will you destroy the whole city? Won't you spare it in order to save the fifty? **25** Surely you won't kill the innocent with the guilty. That's impossible! You can't do that. If you did, the innocent would be punished along with the guilty. That is impossible. The judge of all the earth has to act justly."

....

18.10 *Nine months from now;* or *This time next year.*

See also: 18.2a: Heb 13.2   **18.10:** Rom 9.9

18.18 *through… nations;* or *all the nations will ask me to bless them as I have blessed him.*

See also: 18.12: 1 Pet 3.6   **18.14:** Lk 1.37

26 The LORD answered, "If I find fifty innocent people in Sodom, I will spare the whole city for their sake."

27 Abraham spoke again: "Please forgive my boldness in continuing to speak to you, Lord. I am only a man and have no right to say anything. **28** But perhaps there will be only 45 innocent people instead of fifty. Will you destroy the whole city because there are five too few?"

The LORD answered, "I will not destroy the city if I find 45 innocent people."

29 Abraham spoke again: "Perhaps there will be only forty."

He replied, "I will not destroy it if there are forty."

30 Abraham said, "Please don't be angry, Lord, but I must speak again. What if there are only thirty?"

He said, "I will not do it if I find thirty."

31 Abraham said, "Please forgive my boldness in continuing to speak to you, Lord. Suppose that only twenty are found?"

He said, "I will not destroy the city if I find twenty."

32 Abraham said, "Please don't be angry, Lord, and I will speak just once more. What if only ten are found?"

He said, "I will not destroy it if there are ten." **33** After he had finished speaking with Abraham, the LORD went away, and Abraham returned home.

The Sinfulness of Sodom

19 **1** When the two angels came to Sodom that evening, Lot was sitting at the city gate. As soon as he saw them, he got up and went to meet them. He bowed down before them **2** and said, "Sirs, I am here to serve you. Please come to my house. You can wash your feet and stay the night. In the morning you can get up early and go on your way."

But they answered, "No, we will spend the night here in the city square."

3 He kept on urging them, and finally they went with him to his house. Lot ordered his servants to bake some bread and prepare a fine meal for the guests. When it was ready, they ate it.

4 Before the guests went to bed, the men of Sodom surrounded the house. All the men of the city, both young and old, were there. **5** *They called out to Lot and asked, "Where are the men who came to stay with you tonight? Bring them out to us!" The men of Sodom wanted to have sex with them.

6 Lot went outside and closed the door behind him. **7** He said to them, "Friends, I beg you, don't do such a wicked thing! **8** Look, I have two daughters who are still virgins. Let me bring them out to you, and you can do whatever you want with them. But don't do anything to these men; they are guests in my house, and I must protect them."

9 But they said, "Get out of our way, you foreigner! Who are you to tell us what to do? Out of our way, or we will treat you worse than them." They pushed Lot back and moved up to break down the door. **10** But the two men inside reached out, pulled Lot back into the house, and shut the door. **11** *Then they struck all the men outside with blindness, so that they couldn't find the door.

Lot Leaves Sodom

12 The two men said to Lot, "If you have anyone else here — sons, daughters, sons-in-law, or any other relatives living in the city — get them out of here, **13** because we are going to destroy this place. The LORD has heard the terrible accusations against these people and has sent us to destroy Sodom."

14 Then Lot went to the men that his daughters were going to marry, and said, "Hurry up and get out of here; the LORD is going to destroy this place." But they thought he was joking.

15 At dawn the angels tried to make Lot hurry. "Quick!" they said. "Take your wife and your two daughters and get out, so that you will not lose your lives when the city is destroyed." **16** *Lot hesitated. The LORD, however, had pity on him; so the men took him, his wife, and his two daughters by the hand and led them out of the city. **17** Then one of the angels said, "Run for your lives! Don't look back and don't stop in the valley. Run to the hills, so that you won't be killed."

....

See also: **19.5–8:** Judg 19.22–24   **19.11:** 2 Kgs 6.18
19.16: 2 Pet 2.7

18 But Lot answered, "No, please don't make us do that, sir. **19** You have done me a great favour and saved my life. But the hills are too far away; the disaster will overtake me, and I will die before I get there. **20** Do you see that little town? It is near enough. Let me go over there — you can see it is just a small place — and I will be safe."

21 He answered, "All right, I agree. I won't destroy that town. **22** Hurry! Run! I can't do anything until you get there."

Because Lot called it small, the town was named Zoar.*

The Destruction of Sodom and Gomorrah

23 The sun was rising when Lot reached Zoar. **24** *Suddenly the LORD rained burning sulphur on the cities of Sodom and Gomorrah **25** and destroyed them and the whole valley, along with all the people there and everything that grew on the land. **26** *But Lot's wife looked back and was turned into a pillar of salt.

27 Early the next morning Abraham hurried to the place where he had stood in the presence of the LORD. **28** He looked down at Sodom and Gomorrah and the whole valley and saw smoke rising from the land, like smoke from a huge furnace. **29** But when God destroyed the cities of the valley where Lot was living, he kept Abraham in mind and allowed Lot to escape to safety.

The Origin of the Moabites and Ammonites

30 Because Lot was afraid to stay in Zoar, he and his two daughters moved up into the hills and lived in a cave. **31** The elder daughter said to her sister, "Our father is getting old, and there are no men in the whole world* to marry us so that we can have children. **32** Come on, let's make our father drunk, so that we can sleep with him and have children by him." **33** That night they gave him wine to drink, and the elder daughter had intercourse with him. But he was so drunk that he didn't know it.

34 The next day the elder daughter said to her sister, "I slept with him last night; now let's make him drunk again tonight, and you sleep with him. Then each of us will have a child by our father." **35** So that night they made him drunk, and the younger daughter had intercourse with him. Again he was so drunk that he didn't know it. **36** In this way both of Lot's daughters became pregnant by their own father. **37** The elder daughter had a son, whom she named Moab.* He was the ancestor of the present-day Moabites. **38** The younger daughter also had a son, whom she named Benammi.* He was the ancestor of the present-day Ammonites.

Abraham and Abimelech

20 **1** Abraham moved from Mamre to the southern part of Canaan and lived between Kadesh and Shur. Later, while he was living in Gerar, **2** *he said that his wife Sarah was his sister. So King Abimelech of Gerar had Sarah brought to him. **3** One night God appeared to him in a dream and said: "You are going to die, because you have taken this woman; she is already married."

4 But Abimelech had not come near her, and he said, "Lord, I am innocent! Would you destroy me and my people? **5** Abraham himself said that she was his sister, and she said the same thing. I did this with a clear conscience, and I have done no wrong."

6 God replied in the dream, "Yes, I know that you did it with a clear conscience; so I kept you from sinning against me and did not let you touch her. **7** But now, give the woman back to her husband. He is a prophet, and he will pray for you, so that you will not die. But if you do not give her back, I warn you that you are going to die, you and all your people."

8 Early the next morning Abimelech called all his officials and told them what had happened, and they were terrified. **9** Then Abimelech called Abraham and

1

19.22 _Zoar:_ This name sounds like the Hebrew for "small".

19.31 _the whole world;_ or _this land._

See also: 19.24–25: Mt 10.15; 11.23–24; Lk 10.12; 17.29; 2 Pet 2.6; Jude 7   **19.26:** Lk 17.32

19.37 _Moab:_ This name sounds like the Hebrew for "from my father".

19.38 _Benammi:_ This name in Hebrew means "son of my relative" and sounds like the Hebrew for "Ammonite".

See also: 20.2: Gen 12.13; 26.7

asked, "What have you done to us? What wrong have I done to you to make you bring this disaster on me and my kingdom? No one should ever do what you have done to me. **10** Why did you do it?"

11 Abraham answered, "I thought that there would be no one here who has reverence for God and that they would kill me to get my wife. **12** She really is my sister. She is the daughter of my father, but not of my mother, and I married her. **13** So when God sent me from my father's house into foreign lands, I said to her, 'You can show how loyal you are to me by telling everyone that I am your brother.'"

14 Then Abimelech gave Sarah back to Abraham, and at the same time he gave him sheep, cattle, and slaves. **15** He said to Abraham, "Here is my whole land; live anywhere you like." **16** He said to Sarah, "I am giving your brother a thousand pieces of silver as proof to all who are with you that you are innocent; everyone will know that you have done no wrong."

17-18 Because of what had happened to Sarah, Abraham's wife, the LORD had made it impossible for any woman in Abimelech's palace to have children. So Abraham prayed for Abimelech, and God healed him. He also healed his wife and his slave women, so that they could have children.

The Birth of Isaac

21 **1** The LORD blessed Sarah, as he had promised, **2** *and she became pregnant and bore a son to Abraham when he was old. The boy was born at the time God had said he would be born. **3** Abraham named him Isaac, **4** *and when Isaac was eight days old, Abraham circumcised him, as God had commanded. **5** Abraham was a hundred years old when Isaac was born. **6** Sarah said, "God has brought me joy and laughter.* Everyone who hears about it will laugh with me." **7** Then she added, "Who would have said to Abraham that Sarah would nurse children? Yet I have borne him a son in his old age."

8 The child grew, and on the day that he was weaned, Abraham gave a great feast.

Hagar and Ishmael are Sent Away

9 One day Ishmael, whom Hagar the Egyptian had borne to Abraham, was playing with* Sarah's son Isaac.* **10** *Sarah saw them and said to Abraham, "Send this slave and her son away. The son of this woman must not get any part of your wealth, which my son Isaac should inherit." **11** This troubled Abraham very much, because Ishmael was also his son. **12** *But God said to Abraham, "Don't be worried about the boy and your slave Hagar. Do whatever Sarah tells you, because it is through Isaac that you will have the descendants I have promised. **13** I will also give many children to the son of the slave woman, so that they will become a nation. He too is your son."

14 Early the next morning Abraham gave Hagar some food and a leather bag full of water. He put the child on her back and sent her away. She left and wandered about in the wilderness of Beersheba. **15** When the water was all gone, she left the child under a bush **16** and sat down about a hundred metres away. She said to herself, "I can't bear to see my child die." While she was sitting there, she* began to cry.

17 God heard the boy crying, and from heaven the angel of God spoke to Hagar, "What are you troubled about, Hagar? Don't be afraid. God has heard the boy crying. **18** Get up, go and pick him up, and comfort him. I will make a great nation out of his descendants." **19** Then God opened her eyes, and she saw a well. She went and filled the leather bag with water and gave some to the boy. **20** God was with the boy as he grew up; he lived in the wilderness of Paran and became a skilful hunter. **21** His mother found an Egyptian wife for him.

The Agreement between Abraham and Abimelech

22 *At that time Abimelech went with Phicol, the commander of his army, and

Genesis

1

(left margin note)

21.9 *playing with;* or *making fun of.*
21.9 Some ancient translations *with Sarah's son Isaac;* Hebrew does not have these words.
21.16 *she;* one ancient translation *the child.*

See also: 21.10: Gal 4.29–30   **21.12:** Rom 9.7; Heb 11.18   **21.22:** Gen 26.26

21.6 *laughter:* The name Isaac in Hebrew means "he laughs" (see also 17.17–19).

See also: 21.2: Heb 11.11   **21.4:** Gen 17.12; Acts 7.8

said to Abraham, "God is with you in everything you do. **23** So make a vow here in the presence of God that you will not deceive me, my children, or my descendants. I have been loyal to you, so promise that you will also be loyal to me and to this country in which you are living."

24 Abraham said, "I promise."

25 Abraham complained to Abimelech about a well which the servants of Abimelech had seized. **26** Abimelech said, "I don't know who did this. You didn't tell me about it, and this is the first I have heard of it." **27** Then Abraham gave some sheep and cattle to Abimelech, and the two of them made an agreement. **28** Abraham separated seven lambs from his flock, **29** and Abimelech asked him, "Why did you do that?"

30 Abraham answered, "Accept these seven lambs. By doing this, you admit that I am the one who dug this well." **31** And so the place was called Beersheba,* because it was there that the two of them made a vow.

32 After they had made this agreement at Beersheba, Abimelech and Phicol went back to Philistia. **33** Then Abraham planted a tamarisk tree in Beersheba and worshipped the LORD, the Everlasting God. **34** Abraham lived in Philistia for a long time.

God Commands Abraham to Offer Isaac

22 **1** *Some time later God tested Abraham; he called to him, "Abraham!" And Abraham answered, "Yes, here I am!"

2 *"Take your son," God said, "your only son, Isaac, whom you love so much, and go to the land of Moriah. There on a mountain that I will show you, offer him as a sacrifice to me."

3 Early the next morning Abraham cut some wood for the sacrifice, loaded his donkey, and took Isaac and two servants with him. They started out for the place that God had told him about. **4** On the third day Abraham saw the place in the distance. **5** Then he said to the servants, "Stay here with the donkey. The boy and I will go

over there and worship, and then we will come back to you."

6 Abraham made Isaac carry the wood for the sacrifice, and he himself carried a knife and live coals for starting the fire. As they walked along together, **7** Isaac said, "Father!"

He answered, "Yes, my son?"

Isaac asked, "I see that you have the coals and the wood, but where is the lamb for the sacrifice?"

8 Abraham answered, "God himself will provide one." And the two of them walked on together.

9 *When they came to the place which God had told him about, Abraham built an altar and arranged the wood on it. He tied up his son and placed him on the altar, on top of the wood. **10** Then he picked up the knife to kill him. **11** But the angel of the LORD called to him from heaven, "Abraham, Abraham!"

He answered, "Yes, here I am."

12 "Don't hurt the boy or do anything to him," he said. "Now I know that you honour

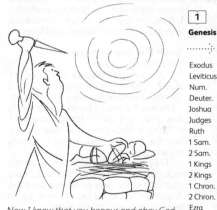

Now I know that you honour and obey God (22.12)

and obey God, because you have not kept back your only son from him."

13 Abraham looked round and saw a ram caught in a bush by its horns. He went and got it and offered it as a burnt offering instead of his son. **14** Abraham named

1

Genesis
........:.

Exodus
Leviticus
Num.
Deuter.
Joshua
Judges
Ruth
1 Sam.
2 Sam.
1 Kings
2 Kings
1 Chron.
2 Chron.
Ezra
Nehem.
Esther
Job
Psalms
Proverbs

21.31 *Beersheba:* This name in Hebrew means "Well of the Vow" or "Well of Seven" (see also 26.33).

See also: 22.1–13: Heb 11.17–19   **22.2:** 2 Chr 3.1   **See also: 22.9:** Jas 2.21

that place "The LORD Provides".* And even today people say, "On the LORD's mountain he provides."*

15 The angel of the LORD called to Abraham from heaven a second time, **16** *"I make a vow by my own name — the LORD is speaking — that I will richly bless you. Because you did this and did not keep back your only son from me, **17** *I promise that I will give you as many descendants as there are stars in the sky or grains of sand along the seashore. Your descendants will conquer their enemies. **18** *All the nations will ask me to bless them as I have blessed your descendants — all because you obeyed my command." **19** Abraham went back to his servants, and they went together to Beersheba, where Abraham settled.

The Descendants of Nahor

20 Some time later Abraham learnt that Milcah had borne eight children to his brother Nahor: **21** Uz the firstborn, Buz his brother, Kemuel the father of Aram, **22** Chesed, Hazo, Pildash, Jidlaph, and Bethuel, **23** Rebecca's father. Milcah bore these eight sons to Nahor, Abraham's brother. **24** Reumah, Nahor's concubine, bore Tebah, Gaham, Tahash, and Maacah.

Sarah Dies and Abraham Buys a Burial Ground

23 **1** Sarah lived to be 127 years old. **2** She died in Hebron in the land of Canaan, and Abraham mourned her death.

3 He left the place where his wife's body was lying, went to the Hittites, and said, **4** *"I am a foreigner living here among you; sell me some land, so that I can bury my wife."

5 They answered, **6** "Listen to us, sir. We look upon you as a mighty leader; bury your wife in the best grave that we have. Any of us would be glad to give you a grave, so that you can bury her."

7 Then Abraham bowed before them **8** and said, "If you are willing to let me bury my wife here, please ask Ephron son of Zohar **9** to sell me Machpelah Cave, which

is near the edge of his field. Ask him to sell it to me for its full price, here in your presence, so that I can own it as a burial ground."

10 Ephron himself was sitting with the other Hittites at the meeting place at the city gate; he answered in the hearing of everyone there, **11** "Listen, sir; I will give you the whole field and the cave that is in it. Here in the presence of my own people, I will give it to you, so that you can bury your wife."

12 But Abraham bowed before the Hittites **13** and said to Ephron, so that everyone could hear, "May I ask you, please, to listen. I will buy the whole field. Accept my payment, and I will bury my wife there."

14 Ephron answered, **15** "Sir, land worth only 400 pieces of silver — what is that between us? Bury your wife in it." **16** Abraham agreed and weighed out the amount that Ephron had mentioned in the hearing of the people — 400 pieces of silver, according to the standard weights used by the merchants.

17 That is how the property which had belonged to Ephron at Machpelah, east of Mamre, became Abraham's. It included the field, the cave which was in it, and all the trees in the field up to the edge of the property. **18** It was recognized as Abraham's property by all the Hittites who were there at the meeting.

19 Then Abraham buried his wife Sarah in that cave in the land of Canaan. **20** So the field which had belonged to the Hittites, and the cave in it, became the property of Abraham for a burial ground.

A Wife for Isaac

24 **1** Abraham was now very old, and the LORD had blessed him in everything he did. **2** He said to his oldest servant, who was in charge of all that he had, "Place your hand between my thighs* and make a vow. **3** I want you to make a vow in the name of the LORD, the God of heaven and earth, that you will not choose a wife for my son from the people here in Canaan. **4** You must go back to the country where I was born and get a wife for my son Isaac from among my relatives."

22.14 *Provides;* or *Sees.*
22.14 *provides;* or *is seen.*

See also: 22.16–17: Heb 6.13–14
22.17: Heb 11.12   **22.18:** Acts 3.25
23.4: Heb 11.9, 13; Acts 7.16

See also: 24.2 *Place… thighs:* This was the way in which a vow was made absolutely unchangeable.

Genesis

1

5 But the servant asked, "What if the young woman will not leave home to come with me to this land? Shall I send your son back to the land you came from?"

6 Abraham answered, "Make sure that you don't send my son back there! **7** The LORD, the God of heaven, brought me from the home of my father and from the land of my relatives, and he solemnly promised me that he would give this land to my descendants. He will send his angel before you, so that you can get a wife there for my son. **8** If the young woman is not willing to come with you, you will be free from this promise. But you must not under any circumstances take my son back there." **9** So the servant put his hand between the thighs of Abraham, his master, and made a vow to do what Abraham had asked.

10 The servant, who was in charge of Abraham's property, took ten of his master's camels and went to the city where Nahor had lived in northern Mesopotamia. **11** When he arrived, he made the camels kneel down at the well outside the city. It was late afternoon, the time when women came out to get water. **12** He prayed, "LORD, God of my master Abraham, give me success today and keep your promise to my master. **13** Here I am at the well where the young women of the city will be coming to get water. **14** I will say to one of them, 'Please, lower your jar and let me have a drink.' If she says, 'Drink, and I will also bring water for your camels,' may she be the one that you have chosen for your servant Isaac. If this happens, I will know that you have kept your promise to my master."

15 Before he had finished praying, Rebecca arrived with a water jar on her shoulder. She was the daughter of Bethuel, who was the son of Abraham's brother Nahor and his wife Milcah. **16** She was a very beautiful young woman and still a virgin. She went down to the well, filled her jar, and came back. **17** The servant ran to meet her and said, "Please give me a drink of water from your jar."

18 She said, "Drink, sir," and quickly lowered her jar from her shoulder and held it while he drank. **19** When he had finished, she said, "I will also bring water for your camels and let them have all they want." **20** She quickly emptied her jar into the animals' drinking-trough and ran to the well

to get more water, until she had watered all his camels. **21** The man kept watching her in silence, to see if the LORD had given him success.

22 When she had finished, the man took an expensive gold ring and put it in her nose and put two large gold bracelets on her arms. **23** He said, "Please tell me who your father is. Is there room in his house for my men and me to spend the night?"

24 "My father is Bethuel son of Nahor and Milcah," she answered. **25** "There is plenty of straw and fodder at our house, and there is a place for you to stay."

26 Then the man knelt down and worshipped the LORD. **27** He said, "Praise the LORD, the God of my master Abraham, who has faithfully kept his promise to my master. The LORD has led me straight to my master's relatives."

28 The young woman ran to her mother's house and told the whole story. **29** Now Rebecca had a brother named Laban, and he ran outside to go to the well where Abraham's servant was. **30** Laban had seen the nose-ring and the bracelets on his sister's arms and had heard her say what the man had told her. He went to Abraham's servant, who was standing by his camels at the well, **31** and said, "Come home with me. You are a man whom the LORD has blessed. Why are you standing out here? I have a room ready for you in my house, and there is a place for your camels."

32 So the man went into the house, and Laban unloaded the camels and gave them straw and fodder. Then he brought water for Abraham's servant and his men to wash their feet. **33** When food was brought, the man said, "I will not eat until I have said what I have to say."

Laban said, "Go on and speak."

34 "I am the servant of Abraham," he began. **35** "The LORD has greatly blessed my master and made him a rich man. He has given him flocks of sheep and goats, cattle, silver, gold, male and female slaves, camels, and donkeys. **36** Sarah, my master's wife, bore him a son when she was old, and my master has given everything he owns to him. **37** My master made me promise with a vow to obey his command. He said, 'Do not choose a wife for my son from the young women in the land of Canaan. **38** Instead, go to my father's people, to my relatives, and choose a wife for him.' **39** And I asked my master, 'What if she will not come with me?' **40** He answered, 'The LORD, whom I have always obeyed, will send his angel with you and give you success. You will get for my son a wife from my own people, from my father's family. **41** There is only one way for you to be free from your vow: if you go to my relatives and they refuse you, then you will be free.'

42 "When I came to the well today, I prayed, 'LORD, God of my master Abraham, please give me success in what I am doing. **43** Here I am at the well. When a young woman comes out to get water, I will ask her to give me a drink of water from her jar. **44** If she agrees and also offers to bring water for my camels, may she be the one that you have chosen as the wife for my master's son.' **45** Before I had finished my silent prayer, Rebecca came with a water jar on her shoulder and went down to the well to get water. I said to her, 'Please give me a drink.' **46** She quickly lowered her jar from her shoulder and said, 'Drink, and I will also water your camels.' So I drank, and she watered the camels. **47** I asked her, 'Who is your father?' And she answered, 'My father is Bethuel son of Nahor and Milcah.' Then I put the ring in her nose and the bracelets on her arms. **48** I knelt down and worshipped the LORD. I praised the LORD, the God of my master Abraham, who had led me straight to my master's relative, where I found his daughter for my master's son. **49** Now, if you intend to fulfil your responsibility towards my master and treat him fairly, please tell me; if not, say so, and I will decide what to do."

50 Laban and Bethuel answered, "Since this matter comes from the LORD, it is not for us to make a decision. **51** Here is Rebecca; take her and go. Let her become the wife of your master's son, as the LORD himself has said." **52** When the servant of Abraham heard this, he bowed down and worshipped the LORD. **53** Then he brought out clothing and silver and gold jewellery, and gave them to Rebecca. He also gave expensive gifts to her brother and to her mother.

54 Then Abraham's servant and the men with him ate and drank, and spent the night there. When they got up in the morning, he said, "Let me go back to my master."

55 But Rebecca's brother and her mother said, "Let her stay with us a week or ten days, and then she may go."

56 But he said, "Don't make us stay. The LORD has made my journey a success; let me go back to my master."

57 They answered, "Let's call her and find out what she has to say." **58** So they called Rebecca and asked, "Do you want to go with this man?"

"Yes," she answered.

59 So they let Rebecca and her old family servant go with Abraham's servant and his men. **60** And they gave Rebecca their blessing in these words:

> "May you, sister, become the mother
> of millions!
> May your descendants conquer the
> cities of their enemies!"

61 Then Rebecca and her young women got ready and mounted the camels to go with Abraham's servant, and they all started out.

62 Isaac had come into the wilderness of* "The Well of the Living One who Sees Me" and was staying in the southern part of Canaan. **63** He went out in the early evening to take a walk in the fields and saw camels coming. **64** When Rebecca saw Isaac, she got down from her camel **65** and asked Abraham's servant, "Who is that man walking towards us in the field?"

"He is my master," the servant answered. So she took her scarf and covered her face.

66 The servant told Isaac everything he had done. **67** Then Isaac brought Rebecca into the tent that his mother Sarah had lived in, and she became his wife. Isaac loved Rebecca, and so he was comforted for the loss of his mother.

Other Descendants of Abraham
(1 Chr 1.32–33)

25 **1** Abraham married another wife, whose name was Keturah. **2** She bore him Zimran, Jokshan, Medan, Midian, Ishbak, and Shuah. **3** Jokshan was the father of Sheba and Dedan, and the descendants of Dedan were the Asshurim, the Letushim, and the Leummim. **4** The sons of Midian were Ephah, Epher, Hanoch,

....

24.62 Some ancient translations *into the wilderness of;* Hebrew *from coming.*